Catherine Marshall

Meeting God at Every Turn

A Personal Family Story

HODDER AND STOUGHTON

LONDON SYDNEY AUCKLAND TORONTO

Scripture quotations identified Moffatt are from *The Bible: A New Translation* by James Moffatt, copyright 1954 by James A. R. Moffatt, and are used by permission of Harper & Row Publishers, Inc.

Scripture quotations identified RSV are from *The Revised Standard Version of the Bible*, copyright 1946, 1952, © 1971, 1973 by the Division of Christian Education of the National Council of Churches of Christ in the U.S.A., and are used by permission.

Scripture quotations identified KJV are from *The King James Version of the Bible*.

Old Testament Scripture quotations identified AMPLIFIED are from *The Amplified Bible, Old Testament*, copyright 1962, 1964 by Zondervan Publishing House, and are used by permission.

New Testament Scripture quotations identified AMPLIFIED are from *The Amplified New Testament*, © 1958 by the Lockman Foundation, and are used by permission.

ISBN 0 340 27155 8

To
The Family—yours and mine,
God's loving gift
to mankind

Acknowledgements

I wish to express my appreciation for the loving, faithful help of my secretary, Jeanne Sevigny, and of Alice Watkins, who have patiently typed and retyped their way through so many revisions of this manuscript; to Gordon Carlson for his copy editing.

My gratitude to my husband, Leonard LeSourd, who did yeoman service in the sorting, selecting, and editing of much of this material; to Elizabeth Sherrill for her fine, sensitive critique; to Marilyn Connell of *Guideposts* magazine for her ideas and suggestions; to my long time friend Gordon Cosby, pastor of the Church of the Saviour, Washington, D.C., for his permission to relate the incident in Chapter Nine.

And how deeply obligated I am to the members of our family, all the way from my mother, age 89, to David Christopher Marshall, age two months, for their tolerance of glass-house living with me; especially for their willingness to share with so many others the inside story of God's gracious dealings with our family.

Catherine Marshall
Boynton Beach, Florida
November 14, 1980

Contents

Foreword

For us, 1980 will always be our "family summer" when we had two weddings and a birth. In two months three new members were added to the family—Susan Scott, who became our son Chester's wife; Philip Lader, who married our daughter Linda; David Christopher, born to Edith and Peter Marshall.

Susan and Chester's wedding was in Chattanooga, Tennessee on August 9, with Susan, blonde and lovely; six bridesmaids; Peter Jonathan Marshall, age six, proudly carrying the rings on a satin pillow as he marched down the aisle beside the petite flower girl; Len as Chester's best man; Jeffrey standing beside him as head groomsman. After that, we took a deep, collective breath and plunged into preparations for the second big event.

In the crowded days preceding Linda's wedding in Washington on September 21, she asked one day for some special time alone with me.

Our talk took place in the upstairs bedroom—Len's and my retreat spot at Evergreen Farm—I, relaxed in one of the two blue lounge chairs, Linda sitting in the low slipper chair, hugging her knees.

Looking at her, I liked what I saw: a slender, lovely woman of thirty-one, her face alive, her blue eyes under her dark lashes full of love. So different from the chunky ten-year-old I had first seen, all knees and elbows, regarding her "new Mommie" with a degree of suspicion. What a long and often tortuous road this daughter and I had traveled. Yet how gloriously God had answered Len's and my prayers for her.

Linda must have been having some of the same thoughts. "Mom, first I'd like you to know how much I appreciate your hanging in there with me all these years. I know I made life hard for you sometimes. Thanks for not giving up on me."

We were silent for a moment, letting the serenity of the room with its pale blue walls, and the green of the rolling pastureland seen through the wide windows make its own oasis for us in the midst of the bustling turbulence of wedding preparations.

"And now I have a request," Linda plunged on. "Do you have any advice for Phil and me? You and Dad haven't had it easy. After over twenty years together, I know you've learned a lot. Is there any way you can summarize all that, give Phil and me some perspective on it?"

"Linda, you astound me," I laughed. "Sum up what your father and I have learned...?" I spread my hands wide, trying to express how unattainable this seemed.

"I know you've written about some of this—various books and articles—things like that, and we've talked before. But you see, Mom, Phil's new to a lot of this, and he's so eager to be a part of this family. He'd like to hear it in a straight line."

I groaned. How could I do what Linda was asking?

Nonetheless, even as the wedding preparations went forward, some part of my mind was pondering Linda's request. One word she had spoken kept playing back to me—*perspective*. Perspective—the vantage point of the years.

Slowly, the conviction surfaced and would not be put down .... Yes, I did have something to share with Linda and Phil, with Susan and Chester, and with others like them. I saw that the road of life I had traveled was no straight line as it so often appears from the wedding altar; rather it had had many a turn and twist and bump and detour. More significantly, I realized that even Christians do not arrive at any goodness or maturity all at once; our life is always a walk. Even on the straight stretches, for me there had often been such heavy fog that I had had to go forward by faith alone that Jesus *was* with me leading the way.

And every time where I had met God had not been on the easy straightaways but on the turns when I had least expected the revelation of His presence.

So after a very memorable wedding was over and the couple had departed on their honeymoon to see the Passion Play in Oberammergau, Germany, then on to England for Phil to introduce his bride to his old haunts at Oxford University, at last there was time to dig in and see what I had to share with Linda and the others.

In my quiet writing workroom I spread out books, letters, scrapbooks, files of magazine articles I had written. Last, I pulled off the bookshelves my Journals, one for each year, dating back to 1934. Such a variety of types of notebooks and bindings! I had begun with a five-year diary allowing four lines per day. No good. The author in me needed more space than that. Then had come a series of dark-green, bound books provided by an insurance company. One page per day. Better. On to larger bound books for the Journals—red, brown, blue.

As I picked up any one of these and dipped in at any page, memories thronged. Inserted between the pages of one was the first love letter Peter had written me after we were engaged. In another, a carefully kept temperature chart from the first weeks of my illness in June 1943. On other pages were the first, awkwardly askew, printed letters of Peter John, four. Often there were my own personal written-down prayers; clippings pasted in; lists; thoughts set down—so many of them. How could I have written so much over the years!

As I browsed through this mass of material at random, to my amazement fresh insights began presenting themselves, kept springing up even out of experiences I have shared in previous books.

In searching for God's purpose—the reasons behind events—I saw that whenever I had come to Jesus stripped of pretensions, with a needy spirit, ready to listen to Him and to receive what He had for me, He had met me at my point of need. *He can make the difference in every human situation.*

The word "impossible" melts away with Him. He knows no defeat; can turn every failure and frustration into unexpected victory. He can reverse a doctor's grim prognosis. With Him a seemingly dark and desolate future becomes a joyous new life.

I know all this to be true because I have lived it. I have met God at moments when the straight road turns ... and He has picked me up, wiped away my tears, and set me back on the path of life.

Catherine Marshall
October 26, 1980

A Word to My Readers

Over the years a recurring theme in letters from the readers of my books has been, "Dear Catherine: Forgive me for calling you by your first name, but through your books I feel that I know you, that you are my friend."

I could receive no greater compliment. So here is a personal message to all these special friends.

In *Meeting God at Every Turn*, I have selected twelve periods in my life where an encounter with the Lord has come at a turning point or during a moment of crisis.

Some of these experiences will be familiar to you. A number I have already written about in books, others in magazine articles; some are told here for the first time. Most of the material from my Journals has never been shared. Those episodes which have been set down previously are retold here because His living Presence along with the passing of time, continues to bring fresh perspective and insight.

Judging from your letters, there has rarely been a time of such desperation and lostness in all parts of the world, in every strata of society. If you are one of those with seemingly inescapable needs in your life, then this book is for you. It is the true story of how God has met me and is still meeting me at every turn. It is the assurance that if He would deal so lovingly with someone like me, then you too can meet Him in a person-to-Person encounter, feel His love for you, and know that He is the answer to every cry of your heart.

C. M.

John Ambrose Wood

I

Our Father Who Art On Earth

For this reason, then,
I kneel before the Father
from whom every family
in heaven and on earth
derives its name and nature....

Ephesians 3:14-15

Our Father
Who Art On Earth

My early childhood was a crazy mixture of exuberant joy interspersed with moments of fear. It was a mystery to me, and certainly must have been to those around me, why I was so shy and fearful.

Assorted odd things alarmed me, such as the dark, mice, spiders, snakes, the nuns in their flowing black habits in the Catholic school across the street, the patched snowman-shaped hole cut by a burglar in the back porch screening, the page in the *Book of Knowledge* picturing Joan d'Arc being burned at the stake. Yet as soon as my father was near, my world was invulnerable.

My dad, the young preacher, John Wood, was tall and very slim, with black hair always neatly combed and soft brown eyes with a glint of mischief in them. And very handsome, I thought. He was gregarious, full of good humor, a father fond of teasing and of practical jokes. Some of the most memorable moments of my early childhood revolve around him.

Until I was seven, I was the only child. Then came my brother, Bob, and 14 months later, my sister, Emmy. Because Dad was a Presbyterian preacher and chose to have his office at home rather than at the church, I saw more of my father than most children do.

Often I would creep into his home office unbidden, but he was never too busy for me. Invariably, he would smile and hold out his arms to receive me. "Girlie—my girlie," he would say.

Even when Father had a guest, he would allow me to sit quietly, silently on his lap while he carried on a leisurely conversation with some church officer or visitor or the young Catholic priest who lived on the next street and often dropped by. Dad's lap always seemed more commodious than Mother's, his arms more firm. For me, those arms were protection and reassurance, warmth, strength and nourishment. In some strange way, the love that flowed between us must have been nourishment for him too.

The setting for those earliest memories was a one-floor white frame home in Canton, a small mid-Mississippi town. This cottage-manse was dwarfed by the red-brick church sitting squarely beside it, overshadowed by huge old oak trees shading both yards. The giant oaks also lined Peace Street in front, creating a tunnel of green through which to walk or drive or bicycle, welcome respite from the cruel Mississippi sun.

My shyness might have led eventually to withdrawal and a feeling of inferiority, for I could not easily admit people to my inner self. Fortunately, this pervading reticence and tendency to hug childish secrets to myself was countered by the way my parents treated me. Since I had "discovered" Robert Louis Stevenson's *A Child's Garden of Verses* and enjoyed the sound of the rhythms and cadences slipping off my tongue, I was encouraged to memorize some of my favorite poems and to recite these to my family.

When Father wanted to chop down the wisteria vine, all but smothering the old coal house in our back yard, and I loudly protested, patiently he listened to my pleas, smiling at the ardor of my appeal. "If you feel that strongly about it..." he said, patting my hand, "I'll just give the wisteria a haircut." And I trotted away satisfied.

When I had progressed in my piano lessons far enough to play simple hymns, Father would sometimes allow me the fun of being the pianist in a small church parlor meeting.

Thus early I was given a sure sense of self-worth, the recognition of my individuality and the surety of being loved and cherished. These are securities that parents can give their children only through their actions.

The other side of such love and attention was that our parents were still the authority figures in our home. They let us children know that we were held responsible for our own conduct. Nor were we allowed to give up easily on tasks or lessons which we considered difficult. Their attitude was always, "We'll help you where help is really needed. Between us, *nothing* is too hard."

That included a regular Sunday afternoon session of memorizing the questions and answers of *The Catechism for Young Children,* followed by the misnamed *Shorter Catechism of the Westminster Assembly.* (Actually, the "Shorter" is considerably longer!) There would be a prize at the end of the long trek of memorization, but finished it must be.

A futile religious exercise? Not a bit of it! Couched in the chiseled English of another century, beautiful in its clarity and simplicity, this laid a very right base for those all-important questions about life and death, about God and our relationship to Him.

Q. What is God?

A. God is a Spirit, infinite, eternal and unchangeable, in His being, wisdom, power, holiness, justice, goodness and truth.

Q. What is the chief end of man?

A. Man's chief end is to glorify God, and to enjoy Him
  forever....

That last idea was startling to me. From some of the
pictures and tales in my Bible story books, the Jehovah of
the Old Testament seemed stern and unapproachable except for someone like Moses or Abraham. This God thundered from Sinai and asked for sacrifices. His fierce anger
destroyed large cities like Tyre and Nineveh, once flooded
the whole world and drowned everyone in it except for
Noah and his family.

Yet here was the Catechism telling me that God was not
to be feared but actually *enjoyed!* That I would have to
ponder long and deeply.

One day I asked my parents, "How can I love someone
I'm afraid of?"

"Because He loves you," came Dad's reply. "Remember
that Bible verse on your Sunday School folder just last
week, 'We love Him because He first loved us.' He loved
you before you even knew He was there."

"But I can't feel it, or hear any words, or see a face full
of love like I see your face, Dad."

"That's exactly why Jesus came down to earth, to tell
us and show us that the Father in heaven is all love, is
made of love. Jesus liked to say that even the best human
father couldn't be half as loving or kind or generous as the
heavenly Father."

Seeing doubt on my face, Dad added gently, "Sometimes I have to punish you or Bob or Em when you have
disobeyed or are clearly in the wrong. I'd be a poor father
to you if I *didn't* correct you. But that doesn't mean that
you're afraid of me, does it?"

Looking into those warm brown eyes, I saw only love
beyond measure and as always, that glint of humor. Certainly I could trust my earthly father. But God was still
vague, up in heaven somewhere. I still wasn't sure where
I stood with Him.

So I went my blithe way reveling in the freedom to roam
in an outdoor world of never-ending delights. In the midst
of this, the fact that our family had little money mattered
to me not at all. We had each other, and we had fun
together. And so many years later, I have only to turn my
memory loose, instantly to recapture the feel of a small
child's fresh, sharp joy of sight and sound and touch and
smell.

To others the yard around our cottage-manse where I
played with the boys next door and with my friends Tay
and Laurie-Bodie, may have seemed ordinary enough; to
me, it was my very own Eden fresh from the heavenly
Father's hand. How could there be anywhere a more delicious fragrance than the southern honeysuckle that rioted
over all the fences? And not only fragrance, but taste. Pick
a blossom, delicately bite off the stem end of it, suck out
the delicious honey. No wonder the bees loved it! What
bliss in the spring to hunt for the first white bells of snow-
drops amongst the green foliage and to bury my nose in
the first hyacinths. How could my eyes absorb enough of
the beauty of the purple wisteria vine I had persuaded
Father to save? Had anyone before me ever really felt the
enchantment of bare feet on the thick carpet of moss under
the oaks? Or of perching high in the leafy bower of the fig
tree, feeling as free as the birds that darted and wheeled
and sang all around me? Did grownups really know the
succulent deliciousness on the tongue of plump, juicy figs
picked from the tree and eaten in that leafy fairyland?

Years later I would read the Genesis account of how the
Creator looked with approval upon each day's handiwork
after He had flung the galaxies of stars and planets into
space. Then He created the creatures, the fish and fowl,
the trees and herbs—and always He "*saw that it was good.*"
And reading it was like an echo out of my own deep spirit.
Of course it was good—every flower, every fragrance,
every fluffy, drifting cloud and singing bird. Not only

"good" but glorious. My child's heart had known it all along.

But my private Eden also bore the unmistakable mark of my earthly father. It was Dad who constructed an outsized sandbox for me where my playmates and I spent endless hours building elaborate sand castles.

It was he who built a see-saw, sturdier and longer than any to be found in any store. We children always marveled that everything Dad built was big and heavy, meant to last a lifetime.

And the swing! Quickly we learned to stand and "pump": begin slowly, bend the knees in rhythm with the swinging. Make it go higher, higher, up and down. Now again, swishing through the air, until finally the jerk of the chains told us that the swing had gone as high as it could. Then "let the cat die."

There were joys awaiting me inside our home too. As in many older, deep-South homes, the 10-foot wide, cool, center hall ran the length of our house with the rooms on either side opening off it. This gallery-corridor was the favorite site for games. All of these revolved around my father. What was pure gold were the hours he spent with us children playing *Parcheesi*, caroms, checkers, dominos, *Rook, Old Maid*, jackstraws, jacks or putting together countless jigsaw puzzles. For some reason, Mother could never get the hang of games, so she would mend or sew or read while Dad and I and anyone else we could pull in, battled tenaciously to win. Father was a sharp competitor, and he never gave us children any quarter because we were small. We liked it that way, for when we won, the taste of victory was all the sweeter.

Often I would walk to the grocery store with Dad for some needed item that Mother had forgotten to put on the grocery list. Sometimes of an afternoon when he was going "calling," Father would take me along, and I would ride proudly beside him in the front seat of the old Dodge touring car which we were able to afford only in the latter part of my childhood. In these situations however, there was the discipline of having to wait out each call alone in the car.

I enjoyed standing or sitting on the floor beside my father, talking to him as I watched him making repairs around the house. He was a good carpenter and painter, even bricklayer and stonemason, with an adequate knowledge of plumbing and electricity. I, and my brother and sister after me, were the recipients of our father's varied skills in a procession of bookcases for our bedrooms, wagons, clubhouses, croquet and basketball courts lighted for night use, goldfish ponds, doll houses and furniture.

It must have been the security of Dad's presence that made his office the most lived-in room in successive manse-homes in Mississippi, the eastern panhandle of West Virginia, and the eastern shore of Virginia. The study was always lined with open bookshelves floor to ceiling. A comfortable leather Morris chair with wide arms sat in the corner just within arm's reach of *The Book of Knowledge*, a beautiful set of Stoddard's *Lectures* on travel, *The Book House*, *The Harvard Classics*, McLaren's *Commentaries on the Scriptures*, along with novels, reference books and innumerable theological books.

Everywhere we moved—from Greenville, Tennessee, to Umatilla, Florida, to Canton, Mississippi, to Keyser, West Virginia—Father's capacious roll-top desk came along, always with a typewriter on a stand beside it. There would be two or three ample rockers in the room, ferns on stands, and in the winter, narcissi and hyacinth bulbs sitting in a sunny window in bowls of water and pebbles to produce a succession of blossoms and fragrance during the snowy months. A canary in its cage and frequently, pans of Mother's feather-light rolls rising on the hot air register completed the coziness of the room.

It was here that the family always gathered after the evening meal while we children worked on our school lessons. Sitting in the Morris chair or at one of the pull-out leaves of Father's desk or sprawled on the floor, we were surrounded by plenty of study helps. Dad subscribed to several magazines, and he always had catalogues from which we children could order books, for our town rarely had a bookstore. All our *National Geographics* were saved for school work, and a cupboard was crammed full of past issues. We were free to cut and paste them as illustrative material for school papers or exhibits.

Dad was never too busy to stop and answer some question about our school work or to help us assemble the material for a product map for a geography lesson, or to hold the book and listen while we recited some memory work for next day's lesson.

My father, of course, had his weaknesses. He could be stubborn. A case in point: the episode of the flamethrower. Fond of tools and gadgets, he was often tempted to spend too much of his meager salary on such things. Since the West Virginia house had a large yard with much lawn, he had treated himself to a power mower. Then soon after that he saw a flamethrower advertised and conceived the idea that a flamethrower was just what he needed. Apparently the War Department had overbought on flamethrowers and was anxious to unload a few.

Mother was annoyed at the idea. "What on God's green earth do you want such a thing for? You know perfectly well we haven't any money to spend on silly things like that."

Father looked wounded. He always looked wounded when anyone of us questioned his judgment about buying gadgets.

"The flamethrower is *exactly* what I need for getting rid of the tall weeds in fence corners," he retorted, "and I *am* going to buy it." With that he stalked off.

Buy it he did. We still have the flamethrower in the family. We also still have weeds.

Then there was his volatile temper. How vividly we remember the time my brother Bob was helping Dad string the Christmas lights over the front door when father's thumb accidentally slipped into the live socket.

Out came the thumb and out of Dad's mouth poured forth some startling, unclergymanlike words. Then Dad glared down from the ladder.

"Son," he said solemnly, "forget that I said that."

Bob never did, of course. Not only that, in later years he told me, "From that moment, I loved and respected Dad more than ever. He was not too 'good' to be human."

Nor could any of us forget the Sunday morning when Bob and Em mischievously created a minor crisis.

During the week before this Sunday, the two children made the rounds of the neighborhood begging empty 15-pound lard cans. Carefully, they neglected to report to our parents how the empty cans were to be used.

Sunday morning our preacher-father was all dressed for church—black hair slicked down, white suit, white shoes—his only pair of shoes not at the repair shop. Since he enjoyed wearing a flower in his buttonhole, Father went out to the garden to select one.

A half minute later we heard a howl. Then red-faced, he stomped into the house with a switch broken off the privet hedge to punish the culprits. It seemed that Bob and Em had filled several lard cans with water and sunk them in strategic places in the flower garden. Over these homemade booby traps they had neatly laid twigs, then a few tufts of grass. Father had walked into one of the traps set in the middle of the garden path. That Sunday Father preached with a wet left foot while two of his children listened with smarting legs.

But Dad was always fair in administering punishment. We knew he loved us even while he was chastizing us. There was no inconsistency with what he preached from the pulpit and the way he dealt with us as the head of the house.

It wasn't that my father was eloquent in the pulpit. He was an average preacher with only a mild interest in theology. His forte was people. He loved them and enjoyed mixing with them, friends and strangers alike. He was easy to be with and had a knack for finding a just-right conversational meeting ground with all manner of folk.

One of my favorite stories is about how Dad went down into the railroad yards near our home in Keyser, West Virginia, to seek out a new member of his congregation. Although our town was close to coalmining territory, Keyser's only industry was the Baltimore and Ohio Railroad's roundhouse and shops. It was in one of the B & O's enormous roundhouses that the Reverend Wood found his man at work.

"Can't shake hands with you," said the man apologetically. "They're too grimy."

John Wood reached down to the ground and rubbed his hands in coal soot. "How about it now?" he said, offering an equalized hand.

And so at an early age I knew I could trust my earthly father. But I resisted the sermons that urged us to surrender our lives to a faraway God. What did that mean? The idea of spending all my time praying, reading the Bible, and talking about God did not appeal to me at all.

When the evangelist Gypsy Smith, Jr., came to hold services in our town, I went with curiosity, but little more. A large tent was pitched on a vacant lot near the town limits. It did not prove large enough to hold the crowds that flocked there. On a platform of raw wood from which the resin still oozed, sat the massed choirs gathered from all the churches. Their favorite anthem was the spirited "Awakening Chorus":

> The Lord Jehovah reigns, and sin is backward hurled!
> Rejoice! Rejoice! Rejoice!

The "rejoicings" vibrated so shrilly that they raised goosebumps along my spine. As the congregation sang, the waving arms of the music director beat out the rhythms of hymns like:

Stan-ding on the prom-i-ses of Christ my king...

or:

Sing them o-ver a-gain to me, Won-der-ful words of
life...

Each time we collectively took a breath, the pianist
would run in scales, chords and flourishes marvelous to
my childish ears.

Then came the preaching—so dynamic that decades
later Gypsy Smith's thundering sermon on Samson still
reverberates in my ears. The word-pictures were vivid:
Samson, blessed of God with great strength through his
hair, succumbed to fleshly temptations and was delivered
into the hands of his enemy, the Philistines. His hair was
cut, his strength gone, his eyes cruelly blinded.

Gypsy Smith would lean far over the crude pulpit, paus-
ing from time to time to whip out a handkerchief and wipe
his flushed, perspiring face or to take a drink of water.

Then that final scene in Samson's drama where a re-
pentant Samson, his hair growing back, his strength returning, faced 3,000 Philistines gathered in the great hall
to make sport of him.

It was not to be. With his right hand on one of the two
key pillars supporting the house, his left hand on the
other, Samson bowed himself with all his might, and the
house fell, crushing himself and all his enemies who had
come to taunt him.

"... So the dead which he slew at his death were more
than they which he slew in his life."

The emotion in Gypsy's preaching, steadily mounting, had
transferred itself to the congregation. What did Samson's
story have to do with those of us who were listening?
Selfishness and sensuality brought only destruction, the
evangelist thundered. It would always be so. But each of
us had to decide which road we would travel.

Finally a hush would fall over the tent as the choir sang almost in a whisper,

> "Softly and tenderly Jesus is calling, Calling for you and me..."

"Believe on the Lord Jesus Christ and thou shalt be saved," the evangelist urged.

Soon at the far edge of the tent someone would rise and slowly make his way down the aisle toward the front. Then another person... and another... and another... and another.

The repeated demands of the preacher did not impress me as much as the faces of the people who went forward. There was radiance and joy on those faces. Most of them seemed eager to get to the front where they knelt and wept and prayed and "gave themselves."

At home I asked my parents about the people who had made this act of commitment to God.

"Does this mean that they joined the church?" I asked. I had no problem with this. All kinds of people were joining the church for all kinds of reasons. As far as I could see, it did not seem to affect them much or demand a great deal. I wondered too, had not some of them "gone forward" out of the emotionalism of the moment or even out of fear? Could either be the right motivation?

Dad understood my wonderings behind the questions. Wisely, he answered, "Sure, most of them will join a church. You too will want to do that at the right time. But Catherine, joining the church is only part of it. The important act is the giving of your life to God so that He can use it for good."

I pondered that statement many times during those preteen years. What did it mean to give my life to God? Something deep inside me rebelled against any phony gift. Dad sensed that in me.

"Catherine, you should not join the church until it really means something," he told me one day. "It must mean the gift of yourself to Him."

Later on came that Sunday morning when I sat in church beside my mother (my brother and sister were in Sunday School classes) and watched my father as he conducted the service. My heart was full of love for him in a special way. I could never remember many things he said from the pulpit, but I felt the way God's love was flowing through him for all of us in the congregation.

At the end of the service, rather spontaneously as I recall, Dad issued an invitation for those to come forward who wanted to accept Jesus as the Lord of their life and to be a part of the church fellowship.

And suddenly I felt a stirring inside me. Very gentle. There was no voice or words, just a feeling of great warmth. I loved my father dearly. And I trusted him with all my heart. I loved him so much that I could feel tears forming behind my eyes.

And then came the assurance. All along God had meant for the love of my earthly father to be a pattern of my heavenly Father and to show me the way to make connection with Him.

Following this inner conviction came the sudden urge to act and the will to do it. To my surprise and Mother's, I rose from the pew and walked down the aisle to the front, joining a half dozen or so others.

At first Dad did not see me as the group lined up in a semicircle around the altar. He spoke to us briefly about the step we were taking and was about to pray when he noticed me.

Full recognition flashed into his brown eyes; he knew instantly that my being there was significant. I was presenting the gift of myself, a first step in faith. The resistance to surrender had been broken.

I shall never forget the look on my father's face. Surprise … joy… sudden vulnerability. He stood there for a long moment in front of the altar, looking at me with eyes swimming in tears behind his spectacles. Then he pulled himself together and had us kneel as he prayed.

It was my first encounter with the living God and my heavenly Father. The catechism had said that He had loved me first. So had my earthly father. He must have loved me even before birth while I was in my mother's body.

Not only that, since I could love and trust my earthly father, how much more could I love and trust my Father in heaven—and then, without fear, place my future in His hands.

What joyous reassurance there was in that bedrock fact!

Leonora Whitaker Wood

II

Mother Never Thought We Were Poor

Give, and it shall
be given unto you....
make for yourselves purses
which do not wear out,
and a treasure in heaven that
does not run short....

Luke 6:38; 12:33—ASB

Mother Never Thought We Were Poor

⊷⊶⊷

$\mathbf{W}$hile my father was the one to present God to me as a heavenly Father who tenderly cared
about each one of His children, it was my mother who
showed me how a relationship with Him could change
everyday situations. The lessons God had taught her were
indigenous to the poverty of the first eighteen years of her
life. Either she had to settle down to lack, or find God's
way out of it. The creative approach He gave her has been
of help to countless numbers of people.

Leonora Haseltine Whitaker was born in 1891 and reared
on North Carolina farms, first in Weaverville, later in Bar-
nardsville. When she was eighteen she volunteered to join
Dr. Edward O. Guerrant's mission in the Great Smoky
Mountains of East Tennesse as a schoolteacher. Her experiences there with the mountain people in the Cove,
buried in the mountains seven miles back of Del Rio, Tennessee, later would form the basis of my novel *Christy*.

Mother was taller than average and—judging from family album pictures—the Gibson-girl shirtwaist dresses

made her seem even taller. She had extremely large, expressive blue eyes and an aquiline nose with a piquant tilt at the end. Her chestnut-colored hair was so long that she could sit on it, though she usually wore it pinned up on the top of her head. At a later period she began braiding it, then winding the braids twice around her head in a lovely natural coronet.

Soon after Leonora Whitaker got to the Cove, the mission was in dire straits for funds to meet basic needs. Mother thought and prayed about this, then an idea dropped into her head. Since she had received invitations to speak in nearby Knoxville to the Tennessee University Club and to the women of one of the churches, she felt there was a good chance these organizations would help her meet the mission's emergency. In addition, she planned to call on a Knoxville businessman with a reputation for philanthropy. What followed was an object lesson in how faith and creativity can blend effectively.

For these engagements she was determined not to look like a dowdy mountain missionary who needed to beg for herself as well as for the mountaineers. Since this was the Lord's work, she wanted her appearance to say, "I'm having fun being a missionary. Wouldn't you like to have a part in this adventure too?"

A visit to a beauty parlor was her first step. She emerged with an elaborate hairdo, curls on top, a figure-eight in the back.

Next, in one of the city's best stores, Mother found an enormous black hat with sweeping ostrich plumes. It would be perfect, she decided, with her one good garment—a black broadcloth suit. But the hat was priced at $25—every penny of her salary for one month. She pondered a long time. Should the $25 go directly into the mission fund? Or would buying the hat actually be an investment in the work? Mother bought the hat.

Her blue eyes sparkling with the fun of this feminine adventure, later that day Mother swept into the downtown

offices of Mr. Rush Hazen, a wholesale grocer and phi-
lanthropist. Heads at rows of desks turned to stare. Even
Mr. Hazen stared. In fact, he all but whistled. "You—a
missionary! I don't believe it. Why hasn't somebody
thought of sending out missionaries like you before? What
can I do for you?"

Mr. Hazen did a great deal. Triumphantly, Mother went
back to the mission with enough food and money to keep
boarding students all winter, with the promise of more
money for the future. She also went back more secure than
ever in the conviction that God would supply our every
need if we but ask Him to show the way.

It was at this mission that Leonora Whitaker met John
Wood who had just graduated from Union Theological
Seminary in Richmond, Virginia. They were married in
Asheville, North Carolina when mother was nineteen.

My parents spent the next forty years serving Presbyterian congregations in small communities and living fru-
gally. Yet that did not dampen Mother's creativity a whit.
I remember vividly an especially harsh period—the early
1930s. By that time our family was living in Keyser, West
Virginia. Because his church people were suffering so
much financially, Dad had voluntarily taken three successive cuts in salary. That meant that our family of five barely
scraped along.

Dad received his portion of what had been in the church
collection plates on Sunday night, and it never lasted the
week. Therefore, the Friday or Saturday grocery shopping
had to include an element of acute embarrassment to us
children. Even now I wince at the remembrance of standing beside my father, pretending not to notice, while he
sought out our friend, the grocer, leaned over the counter,
and said in a lowered voice, "If you will let us have this
list of groceries, I'll drop by on Monday to pay you."

During these lean years our family had no car. We children walked or bicycled. Our parents walked, walked

everywhere—for all shopping, to church, to call on parishioners.

Bob and Em and I could joke about Father sometimes receiving a fee of fifty cents for marrying a couple. And we did not mind the fact that we had to go regularly to a neighbor's to read the Sunday funnies since one of our economies was cutting out the Sunday paper. What we *did* mind were some of the clothes we had to wear. I've never forgotten one brown velvet dress Mother made for me out of someone's hand-me-down. The velvet was worn in places, and the chocolate brown was wrong for a young girl. I suffered in silence every time I wore it. And my sister was mortified, she tells me, by never having proper girl's snow togs of her own, always being forced to wear an old pair of her brother's pants as a snowsuit.

We children certainly did not enjoy those depression years, yet no tinge of fear about lack of money ever clouded our home. It never seemed even to have entered Mother's head that we were living through a period of poverty. She went through each difficult day of the depression as though she had some secret bank account to draw from when we were in need—and in a sense she did. But her real secret was an utterly confident inner attitude: always before her was the picture of a healthy, fulfilled family.

Though we did without many things, Mother always provided us with a feeling of well-being. One way she did this was the unique manner in which she contrived to give to others. Out of our meager pantry she would send a sick neighbor a supper tray of something delicious she had prepared—velvety-smooth, boiled custard; feather-light, homemade rolls—served up on our best china and always with a dainty bouquet from our garden.

While Mother always tried to provide her family a balanced diet with plenty of fruit and vegetables, often we went without meat and I cannot recall any luxury foods. The main course for many an evening meal would be french fries and hot biscuits with honey or jam, or salmon croquettes, or fried mush. But we children didn't mind the mush at all—not the way Mother made it: sliced thin, browned crisp, and served with maple syrup.

Mother could also turn fried mush into an occasion by even giving some of *that* away. This happened when she discovered that Mr. Edwards, our wealthy neighbor, was fond of mush. Since his wife never served him such lowly fare, from time to time he would be the grateful recipient of our hot, golden-fried mush. "Poor Mister Edwards," we would intone in mock sympathy to tease Mother.

Only unconsciously were we aware of it, but Mother was providing us constantly with an object lesson in giving. The message: no matter how little you have, you can always give some of it away. And when you can do that, you can't feel sorry for yourself, and you can scarcely consider yourself poor.

But there was even more to it than that. For Mother, giving was an act of faith, and the spiritual principle of giving out of scarcity came as easily to her as if she had invented it. Whenever we saw an old-fashioned pump in a farmyard, we knew what she would tell us: "If you drink the cup of water that's waiting there, you can slake your own thirst. But if you pour it in the pump and work the handle, you'll start enough water flowing to satisfy all our thirsts."

She likened the principle of priming the pump to God's law of abundance: we give, and He opens the windows of heaven and gives to us. It was a law of life, she explained to us children, and as certain to work as that the sun would rise tomorrow.

Mother had not been in Keyser long before she had a dream of helping the destitute of Mineral County, particularly those who lived in one section called Radical Hill, where people lived in tin-roofed shacks along rutted roads strewn with debris.

This was an unusual slum district because it was not on the wrong side of the tracks. It was located in what should have been the town's most beautiful residential district, far away from the railroad. There unbelievable filth was surrounded by gently rolling hills and towering mountains. The "nice" citizens of the town gave the area a wide berth. Yet the children who lived there, often unwashed and with lice in their hair, sat alongside the "nice" children in the public schools.

Mother's first step was to enlist the help of some of the young people of our church to go with her to visit each home and to take a survey of the district. Of some 500 Radical Hill families, she found that only 80 had any connection with any church.

At that juncture Mother offered her services to the county welfare board and to our surprise (but definitely not hers!) was given a job to help improve conditions in any way she could. Day after day, she would send us off to school in our hand-me-downs and our artfully patched clothing, and then she would go off to help what she called "the poor people."

The first thing Mother managed to do was to get the name of that area changed from Radical Hill to Potomac Heights—a new name for a new start, something to renew and lift the spirits. Then an old abandoned hotel was remodeled—partitions torn out, repaired, painted; bathrooms and a kitchen put in. This was for meetings of all kinds, a Sunday school and a weekday nursery school. A health clinic, craft classes, and Mother's own classes in child care and Bible study for teenagers were started. Soon the work was flourishing. Those who had been giving up hope began to take heart because someone cared.

Then one day Mother was told that county funds had run out and that her employment had to be terminated. For only a moment did she give in to discouragement. Then she approached the director of the welfare board. "May I go on working?" she asked.

"But we can't pay."

"I understand," Mother said. "But why should I do for money what I would be willing to do for the love of God and humanity?"

The man stared at her. "What do you mean?"

"I mean," she said resolutely, "that the work must go on, salary or not. Shutting down now would be disastrous."

The director looked incredulous. Then, impressed by Mother's determination, suddenly his tone changed. Standing up, admiration and enthusiasm written on his face, he thrust out his hand. "All right then, of course, go right on working. I'll do something—we'll *all* do something. Somehow we'll get the community behind us."

So day after day Mother would trudge on foot to Potomac Heights, receiving not a nickel for her work. And the work not only prospered, it zoomed as a large task force of enthusiastic teenagers rallied around Mother to help.

Years later I saw on television Kathryn Forbes' warm Swedish-American reminiscences called "*I Remember Mama.*" Her family of five was exactly like ours—one son and two daughters. The youngest daughter, Dagmar, reminded me of our youngest, Em. And like our family on Overton Place, the family on Castro Street knew the same kind of financial stringency. They too lived from weekly payday to weekly payday.

I sensed still another point of similarity. Kathryn Forbes' Mama had a bank account. Each Saturday night as the stacks of coins would be counted out for the landlord, the grocer, for half-soling shoes and school notebooks, there would be great relief when Mama finally smiled. "Is good," she would say. "We do not have to go to the bank."

Mama's bank account was considered to be only for the direst emergencies. By hard work and much cooperation, the family made it through year after year; just knowing that Mama's bank account was there gave them a warm, secure feeling.

Twenty years later when daughter Kathryn Forbes sold her first story, she proudly took the check to Mama. "For you—to put in your bank account."

Then—finally—the truth came out. There never had been a bank account. Mama had hit upon this device because, she explained, "Is not good for little ones to be afraid—not to feel secure."

Suddenly in a blazing revelation it occured to me that my own mother also had a bank account that kept us—her children—from being afraid. Her bank account too was real—as real as the mountain air we breathed and the nourishing bread she baked, as solid as the gold in Fort Knox. Mother's family bank account was her faith in the Lord, her absolute trust that the promise of "give and it shall be given unto you" was as eternal as the mountains around us.

Even by age twelve I had begun to realize that the secret of Mother's strength was directly related to her daily prayer-conversations with God. I watched her go off alone to talk with Him and wondered what it was like to have a real conversation with God. Could you hear His voice? Was His presence and His love something you could actually feel? I had to find out.

At fourteen I was a thin and somewhat awkward-looking girl with too long a neck. I had naturally curly brown hair, usually unruly hair, with very large blue eyes set in pale face. I was a teenager with a head full of question marks, exclamation points, and some ridiculous and implausible dreams. For how could one live with Leonora Wood and settle down to limited horizons?

"You are the beloved children of the King," she never tired of admonishing us. "Each of you is very special to Him, and He has important work for you to do in the world. It's up to you to find His dream for your life. And take warning, our King doesn't fool around with petty stuff. The sky is the limit!"

By the time I entered high school, I had focused down on three major dreams. The first, born in early adolescence, I hugged to myself: Was there any chance that someday I could write books, be a real author?

Then when I was 15 there came a golden moment when two more dreams came into view. It happened early one spring at the home of Mrs. William MacDonald with whom I would sometimes spend the night when her husband had to be away on law cases.

The MacDonald's daughter, Janet, had gone to a college called Agnes Scott—glamorous and far away in Decatur, Georgia, on the outskirts of Atlanta. "Mrs. Mac" talked about how special the college was, how much it had meant in molding Janet's life.

The MacDonald home seemed luxurious to me: real mahogany furniture, a tall grandfather clock whose musical chimes marked the quarter hour...current books, lovely books of history and travel lying about; and they even received the *New York Times* every Sunday.

When I stayed with Mrs. Mac, it was her custom to serve us ice cream at bedtime—more ice cream than I could eat. Then she would tuck me in under an eiderdown in a bed with tall pineapple posts.

How well I remember one particular night when for me, time paused and stood still. "Good night, my sweet," she said as she turned to leave the room.

Then at the door she stopped, half turned, looked at me. "You make quite a picture lying there. One of these days a wonderful man, just the right man for you, is going to come and carry you away. Just you wait!"

Her words, shockingly daring to me, yet standing straight and tall, marched across the room and found permanent lodgement in my mind and heart. At that moment two dreams were planted inside me: to go to Agnes Scott College and to get ready for that wonderful man who would come from far away to marry me.

I did not realize it at the time, but now that I had given my life to God, He was using that perfect time—impressionable adolescence—to reach down and plant in the fertile soil of my girlish heart His big, pure, wonderful dreams. The fulfillment of them would be His work, not mine, but I was to learn that none of those gloriously impossible dreams could come true without the pain of self-realization and growth.

By the time I graduated from high school, the depression was daily dealing our town devastating blows: businesses failing, banks closing, bankruptcies, suicides, almost everyone living on credit. With our family's hand-to-mouth existence, how could there possibly be any money for college?

Already I had been accepted at Agnes Scott. Even though I had saved some money from debating prizes and had the promise of a work scholarship, we were still hundreds of dollars short of what was needed.

One evening Mother found me lying across my bed, face down, sobbing. She sat down beside me. "You and I are going to deal with this right now," she said quietly.

At this point Mother took me into the guest room, and together we knelt beside the old-fashioned, golden oak bed, the one that Mother and Father had bought for their first home. "Catherine, I know it's right for you to go to college," Mother said. "Every problem has a solution. Let's ask God to tell us how to bring this dream to reality."

As we knelt there together, instinctively I knew that this was an important moment, one to be recorded in heaven. We were about to meet God in a more intimate way than at bedtime prayers or during grace before a meal, or in family prayers together in Dad's study, or even as in most of the prayers in church. Mother was admitting me to the inner sanctum of her prayer closet.

In the silence, I quickly reviewed my relationship with this God with whom we were seeking an audience. At the age of nine I had given Him my life. Attendance at Sunday school and church had been regular ever since, little enough to do as the daughter of a preacher, I thought uneasily.

I had prayed many times since that encounter with Him years before, but how real had these prayers been? The truth then struck me—most had been for selfish purposes. I had given so little of myself to Him. I had not really taken much part in Mother's work to transform Radical Hill to Potomac Heights. And with a sinking heart, I remembered all the times I had seen members of the church coming up the front walk only to flee up the back stairs to my room where I could be alone to read and not have to give myself to others in the sharing of their problems.

Scene after scene flashed across my mind's eye of the times I had resented my brother and sister. Whenever they had interfered with what I wanted to do, I had scolded them, avoided them, rejected them. As I thought of the many occasions when my parents had gone without something they needed so that we children could have new clothing, piano lessons, books or sports equipment, I felt more unworthy than ever. And my going to college would call for yet more sacrifices from my parents.

I stole a look at Mother. She was praying intensely but soundlessly, with her lips moving. Then closing my eyes, silently I prayed the most honest prayer of my life to that point. "Lord, I've been selfish. I've taken everything from You, from Your Church and from my parents and given little of myself in return. Forgive me for this, Lord. Perhaps I don't deserve to go to a college like Agnes Scott."

A sob deep in my throat made me pause. I knew what I now had to do. "And Lord, I turn this dream over to

You. I give it up. It's in Your hands. You decide." Now the tears did come!

Those quiet moments in the bedroom were the most honest I had ever spent with God up to that point. I was learning that the price of a relationship with Him is a dropping of all our masks and pretense. We must come to Him with stark honesty "as we are"—or not at all. My honesty brought me relief; it washed away the guilt; it strengthened my faith.

Several days later Dad and Mother decided that by faith, I should go ahead and make preparations for Agnes Scott. They felt strongly that this was right and that the Lord would soon confirm it. I was not so sure. God had convicted me of my selfishness. Perhaps He wanted me to give up college and serve Him in some other way.

Days passed, then weeks. Then one day Mother opened a letter and gave a whoop of joy. "Here it is! Here's the answer to our prayers."

The letter contained an offer from a special project of the federal government for Mother to write the history of the county. With what I already had, her salary would be more than enough for my college expenses.

Once again, Mother's very real bank account had provided the necessary provision at a time of need. From those hours each day spent alone with Him had come her supreme confidence that He would always provide out of His limitless supply. How often she had told us children, "And don't forget, He will never, never let us outgive Him."

Out of this solid wealth, this certainty, Mother could always afford to give to others, not just material things, but showering sparks of imagination, the gleam of hope, a thrust of courage—qualities that provided more substance than the coin of any realm and which opened the door for fulfillment in many a life she touched.

Catherine at 16

III

My God
Was Too Small

O Lord, You have searched me
and have known me....
Your (infinite) knowledge
is too wonderful for me;
it is high above me,
I cannot reach it....

Psalm 139:1,6—Amplified

My God Was Too Small

∞

Travel from West Virginia to Atlanta, Georgia, for my first semester at Agnes Scott was overnight by train. There was not enough money for a Pullman berth, so I sat up all night in the day coach. But I discovered a way to avoid these sleepless, uncomfortable nights to and from college—make a friend of the conductor. If there was still an empty berth at midnight, he would let a passenger have it for a few dollars.

This need for careful husbanding of money dominated my four years of college during the depression years of the 1930s. My parents stretched their resources to the limit to keep me there with each semester's payment of tuition a cliff-hanger of suspense for me. Any delay of payment brought a summons from Mr. Tart, the college treasurer (aptly named, I always thought), with a resultant surge of panic inside me.

Upon arrival on the campus, I was immediately at home with the ancient magnolia trees, as in my Mississippi childhood, and was soon reveling in the mysterious beauty of

Georgia nights when a soft breeze blew from the south. I discovered grits again and southern accents and Atlanta's Peachtree Street. College life turned out to be a kaleidoscope of bull sessions and truth sessions, hard studying, often a set or two of tennis of an afternoon as a change of pace from long hours in the library, fire drills, endless hair washings and waiting for letters and checks from home. There were dates (since greater Atlanta burgeoned with men's schools), writing and typing papers, the constant jangling of dorm telephones and memorable after-lights-out feasts with boxes from southern homes—fried chicken, potato chips, beaten biscuits, salted pecans, spice cake.

As freshmen we were quickly plunged into "Rat Week." This involved wearing a dress backwards, shoes which did not match, six curlers in our hair and a dab of cold cream on each cheek in the shape of an "F." It also involved crawling whenever we encountered a sophomore.

I found that Agnes Scott girls liked to call themselves "Hottentots" and that the school song, when accompanied by a solemn, full-robed and hooded academic procession, could give me girlish goose pimples.

I discovered the spot on the quadrangle, somehow connected with the college heating plant, which always spouted steam. And I saw that at any evening of the year, the setting sun could turn the ivy on the ancient walls of Main Building to glistening, shining magic.

Gradually, as the weeks passed, I became aware of campus personalities: Dr. J. R. McCain, the college president, who always had time to talk to any girl and whose first pride was Agnes Scott's rapidly rising star in the academic world. Yet he boasted that these high scholastic standards did not subtract from the femininity and marriageability of the women Agnes Scott turned out. Did not 80 percent of Hottentots get married? Was not this a higher percentage than any of the large women's colleges in the East could boast? From time to time Dr. McCain would announce the latest revised matrimonial figure to his girls.

This seemed to please him as much as the list of those who had just made Phi Beta Kappa.

Then there was Dr. Henry Robinson, head of the mathematics department—a math genius but almost equally interested in matchmaking and the then much-debated cause of Prohibition. Dr. Robinson was to play a key role in my dating life at Agnes Scott.

There was Miss Hopkins, the college dean—"Hoppy" we called her privately. She was incalculably patrician; her dress, her walk and her manner were reminiscent of a bygone century. She wore her gray hair in the pompadour style of the early 1900s.

Virginia was my blonde, beautiful roommate. She knew how to use make-up in a professional manner—pancake foundation, eye shadow, mascara, eyebrow pencil. I struggled hard not to envy her. The struggle capitulated and faded into wistfulness when I allowed myself to think of her year's supply of cosmetics—and in all the largest size bottles and jars too. To this day, a whiff of *Evening in Paris* perfume reminds me of Virginia.

Our closets were side by side. On my side, the clothes included a few carefully selected simple dresses and blouse and skirt combinations. Virginia's side held not only a complete school wardrobe, but a black beaver coat to set off her blonde loveliness, a stone marten scarf, many dinner and evening dresses. She always made the beauty section of the Agnes Scott Annual; wherever she went, masculine heads turned.

I watched from a distance; prodded myself with reminders that I was fortunate to be in college at all—wardrobe or no wardrobe; fed myself platitudes that girls could not live by bread (or stone marten scarves) alone, though I often kept wondering what they *did* live by.

Scarcely a week went by during these four years of college that I did not agonize over my finances. Every penny was important; seldom were there extra funds for entertainment or side trips. Once I needed $15 to participate in a college debate against the debating team of England's Oxford University. I did not have it, nor did my parents. My roommate might have loaned it to me, but I was too proud to ask. Having been selected as one of two out of the whole student body for this event, to have to decline because of sheer poverty seemed too humiliating to bear.

At the last minute my parents came through; how they raised the money I do not know to this day.

During the spring of my freshman year came an experience which turned out to be one of the hinges upon which life turns. The English professor, Dr. Emma May Laney, had given us a choice of several authors to research. One name in the list I had never heard of—Katherine Mansfield, the New Zealand short story writer. The assignment was to be a definitive term paper on "our" author. The paper would decide most of our second semester grade.

Curious about Katherine Mansfield, I chose her and chose better than I knew. After reading several volumes of her short stories, I came upon her *Journal*. Passage after passage spoke to something buried deep in me and awakened a response: the way Katherine Mansfield fingered life, rolled it on her tongue so that not one but a dozen taste buds savored it. She had been as a little girl seeing inside everything, from a gull lighting on the water, to a crushed violet in the grass, to the plop of a hard little pear falling from a tree at the bottom of the garden, to watching her playmate, Kezie, "make a river down the middle of her porridge" and then helping her "eat the banks away"; to a little bird sitting on the branch of a tree "sharpening a note"—seeing it all with guileless round eyes, saying to us, "See! New shoes!"

Preparing for the term paper was not work, it was the breath of life. I had discovered pure gold, and I reveled in it. Into a notebook I copied lines from her *Journal* that I especially liked:

Fairylike, the fire rose in two branched flames like the
golden antlers of some enchanted stag.

And the day spent itself . . . The idle hours blew on it
and it shed itself like seed.

She was the same through and through. You could go
on cutting slice after slice and you knew you would
never light upon a plum or a cherry or even a piece of
peel. . .

The sun shone through the windows and winked on
the brass knobs of the bed . . .

They slung talk at each other across the bus . . .[1]

When I turned in the term paper, I had a good feeling
about it. Thus I was quite unprepared for what followed.

A week or so later, I was summoned to the professor's
office. Miss Laney was a fine teacher, but upon occasion
she could have an acid tongue. All of the acid was showing
that day.

"This could not be your original work," she hurled at
me, her pencil jabbing at the Katherine Mansfield paper
before her on the desk. "This paper has Miss Mansfield's
style all over it." With her eyes flashing fire and her mouth
drawn into a straight line, Miss Laney delivered a definitive lecture on the dangers, horrors, and gross dishonesty
of plagiarism.

I burst into tears, too distraught to do anything but stam-
mer, "I didn't mean to copy her style. I just wrote what
I felt."

"But the paper reads as if Miss Mansfield wrote it. It's
excellent, but I don't see how you..." She stopped, not
knowing quite how to tell me that it was too good to be
the work of a college freshman.

Strange, but I have not the slightest recollection of what
grade I was finally given for this paper. I had enjoyed

writing it so much that the grade was no longer the point. Rather, the work had become an experience in self-discovery. I had stumbled upon my special spot. It felt right— where I belonged.

As I painfully mulled over the professor's accusation in the weeks and months that followed, several conclusions emerged. My term paper had been unusual enough for a college freshman to make Miss Laney suspicious. Did I then dare to hope that perhaps, just perhaps, those glimmering, girlhood dreams of someday being an author might be an authentic dream?

And if the charge of plagiarism had arisen because I was unusually sensitive to the style of the author I was reading, I would have to be careful about this in the future. Years later I would be making this point in writers' workshops: every writer must put himself under sharp discipline as to what he reads while writing original material. It won't do to read Hemingway while one's own book is in progress and end up with Hemingwayish copy!

It was in the spring of my freshman year that I first heard the name Peter Marshall mentioned. He was the pastor of Westminster Presbyterian Church there in Atlanta. "A really good preacher," one of the upperclassmen told us, "Scottish and very handsome." Some of my classmates were going regularly to hear him preach, but an hour's ride by streetcar into Atlanta meant time and money I was loathe to spend.

When I finally did go to hear this young Scotsman preach, I was enchanted. I found Peter Marshall to be a tall, well-built man with the broad shoulders of a football player (he would have said "soccer player") camouflaged by his Geneva gown. His hair, which had been very blond, was turning darker. It was curly, never slicked down as

my father's had been. His face was handsome in a rugged
sort of way.

He seemed thoroughly at home in a pulpit. While he
preached, he frequently used gestures, but they were
never strained or artificial. Most of his emphasis was made
with his voice—an extraordinarily resonant speaking voice,
more flexible and dramatic than my father's, with the
added delight of a clear, precise British diction garnished
with his Scottish burr. There was also a marked poetic
streak in his prayers and his sermonizing. As Peter stood
in the pulpit, I, and no doubt others like me, saw him
against a composite backdrop of Edinburgh Castle, John
Knox, skirling bagpipes, and the renowned 51st Division,
all with a touch of heather thrown in.

But there was something even more appealing. Here
was a man who knew his Lord, spoke of Him as his Friend,
shared intimate experiences of His guidance and help. This
was the first time I had heard preaching that brought us,
Peter's congregation, into contact with a present-day Jesus. Every bit of it touched something deep in my spirit.

By the middle of my sophomore year I had begun filling
notebooks with my reactions and observations about my
life at Agnes Scott. This entry was significant:

> I am awfully blue this morning for some unexplain-
> able reason. It must be that let-down feeling after all
> my exams. They were simply awful. I wonder if other
> people suffer as much as I do over them.
>
> I am tired all over. Mentally, physically, spiritually.
> I am lazy spiritually. I would like to know God really—
> not in the abstract. But I don't seem to want to badly
> enough to do anything much about it. I can't fathom
> myself. Perhaps someday—but it's always someday.

The next Sunday I went to hear Peter Marshall preach
and wrote:

> Today was glorious. At breakfast it looked like rain,
> but then the sun came out. While we were waiting for

the streetcar in town, it sprinkled a few big drops. They were like pearls in the face of the sun.

I don't know what's the matter with me. Perhaps I'm simply in a romantic frame of mind these days, but that man Peter Marshall does something to me! I would give anything I own to meet him.

A month or so later I wrote this item in my Journal:

Went to Sunday school and church at Westminster. After Peter had made his talk, he said he didn't know everyone in the class and couldn't we have a social to get acquainted? He said he wanted to meet some of us before all of us had a chance to get married. And then the funny part of it was that he *actually* blushed!

I had the strange and giddy feeling today that it was this particular morning that Mr. Marshall really noticed me for the first time. I could tell by the way he looked and smiled at me. It must have been my new blue hat, which *was* very becoming. . .

Soon I began saving clippings about Peter Marshall that kept appearing in the Atlanta papers, for this young preacher, still in his early 30s, was already making his mark on Atlanta: "A young Scottish preacher with native jargon and impressive dramatic personality... If ever we saw greatness in a man, they are in Peter Marshall. Yet there's an odd boyish shyness about him too... A charming young Scot with a silver tongue... Gay, brilliant, witty."

But reading comments like this, I knew that the elements of "greatness" in this man were not in his wit or his dynamic personality. Rather, in the indisputable fact that under the impact of Peter's praying and preaching, God was becoming real to those who listened. While he led them in worship, God was no longer a remote, theological abstraction but a loving Father who was interested in each individual, who stooped to man's smallest need.

My girlish heart was not the only part of me affected by Peter Marshall. My hunger for excellence was stirred by the quality of his preaching. Even more important, he pricked my spiritual consciousness deeply. Several entries in my journals that spring reflected this:

> I have come to a crisis in my life. It's very easy for me to see how people can lose their so-called religion when they have gotten enough education to make them think at all, particularly if their religion is simply an inheritance or a habit. I'm afraid this is happening to me; I have had no real, vital religious experience. God does not seem real to me. I believe in God now mostly because of people I know—a very few people—like Peter to whom religion is a vital, living thing.
>
> I can't go on like this. I know there must be something to religion, else all of life would be meaningless. Sometimes it is to me. People hurry and bustle and strive, failing to see the beauty around them. Their eyes are on material consideration wholly. We die, and apparently it is all over. I wonder what I was born for after all. *I must know.*

Then a few weeks later, this entry:

> Spring is so beautiful. All the trees are out now, a tangy fresh green. On the way to Decatur I saw pink honeysuckle and lilacs and the air is filled with the fragrance of wisteria. The earth is brown and wet and springy, full of the promise of better things—the hope of life and eternity.
>
> Yet amid all this exquisite beauty, the world is also full of sordid, ugly things. My trip to the University of Georgia was so disheartening. The students there live what seems to me to be superficial and meaningless lives, drinking, always with cigarettes dangling from their lips, gossiping and saying nothing when they *do* talk. None of them ever seem to study. Why do they go to college anyway?
>
> There has got to be something more to life than this, some real purpose. What is *my* purpose? I don't think I've found it. I want my life to be so full. I want to be

able to love and laugh and live and help others to the depth of my capacity.

That summer, still unable to get Peter Marshall out of my thoughts, I put myself through a crash course on Scotland, Scottish history—everything Scottish. Perhaps then I could understand better this Britisher whose background appeared to be so different from mine and who was so much older. Through careful questioning of my parents, I found that all my ancestors had emigrated from the British Isles. I made a bibliography of 37 books on Scotland and pored over some like H. V. Morton's travel account *In Search of Scotland*, Ian MacLaren's sentimental *Beside the Bonny Briar Bush*, Sir Walter Scott's *Minstrelsy of the Scottish Border*, Boswell and Johnson's gutsy account of *A Journey to the Western Isles*. And as I read, many times that summer I marveled at how strong the call of the blood can be for us Americans whose roots are across the sea.

And yet—to what purpose all this reading? Preparation for—what? The end of that summer became a time of sober reassessment. In college I was seeking a base on which to build my life. My mind hungered to be stretched. Yet there were those who had warned me about this: "Watch it! A lot of young people lose all their religious faith in college."

True. And I was vulnerable, coming to college from a traditional Christian upbringing. My concept of God was well-defined and structurally circumscribed. Despite that, the idea world and the learning process were proving to be such an intoxicant that I knew I would have to guard against intellectual gluttony. My strengths and weaknesses were obvious to me: courses in mathematics and science would be agony; those in English, history, philosophy, the arts, speech, music, a joy—and would bring out all my effort and skills.

Then where was God in all this? To my surprise, He was everywhere. Not so much in Religion 101-102, or courses on Old Testament and New Testament. These I found dull, almost stultifying. Especially with the professor who, in his effort to seem liberal and broadminded to us college students, offered us outlandishly contorted, naturalistic explanations for Old Testament miracles. I had respect neither for the far-out theories nor for the prof's too-eager desire to please his students.

But I did see God in the intricate marvels of mathematics, in the inconceivable vastness and complexity of all His creation as I glimpsed it in the sciences, in His footprints through the history of empires and nations and the lives of the men and women who had made history—He was everywhere. Even Comparative Religion proved no threat. Truth was and is truth—indivisible. Bits and pieces of His truth, as much as mens' minds were open to receive, were in all religions of the world. I was learning to assess and to think, and then how to allow Him to help me sort out truth from error.

Already I knew that I need never be afraid of using my mind, for at every point of discovery God came running to meet me, always bigger than my mind, ever out ahead of the greatest scientist, the most eminent doctor, the finest historian. Yes, my God had been too small. Those who had warned me had been wrong. He had given me the mind; His desire was that I use every atom of it.

Thus, the goal of excellence was before me every day of my college life. In fact, it has been in all of my life before and since. Always I have been fascinated, ecstatic over sheer brilliance and quality in writing, in the arts, in scholarship. The question was always before me: How could I throw my ability so totally into a work at hand so as to reach the absolute limit of my capacity? At Agnes Scott I hoped to find the answer.

By the time I returned to college for my junior year, I had decided that allowing myself to be moonstruck over

Peter Marshall was pathetic immaturity. He had made God more real to me; that was all to the good. But I made a firm resolve to be more grown-up about the situation that fall. I would attend Westminster Church occasionally to hear Peter preach, but date men from Emory, Georgia Tech, Columbia Seminary and other nearby colleges. Most of all I would concentrate on my courses, pursue excellence. Maybe a teaching career would be right for me.

As for romance, that might have to wait—for a long time.

Peter Marshall

IV

Romance

Now the Lord God said,
It is not good
(sufficient, satisfactory)
that the man should be alone....
....for love (springs) from God
....for God is love.

Genesis 2:18,
I John 4:7,8—Amplified

Romance

⸙

I returned to Agnes Scott College the fall of my junior year to find a report circulating that Peter Marshall was engaged to be married.

True or not, this reinforced the resolve I had made at the last of the summer: I would be friendly but altogether casual with Peter. There *was* something ridiculous about a soon-to-be 20-year-old college student fancying herself in love with a 32-year-old bachelor-preacher who had captured so many other female hearts in the Atlanta area and who was already becoming well-known for his marriage counseling.

But why does he single me out with his eyes so much when he preaches? I asked myself.

"A dozen other women probably think the same thing," my logical mind snapped back.

The thoughts retorted, *But then why all that special attention after church? Having his secretary, Ruby Coleman, intercept me to tell me that he wants to drive me back to Decatur?*

I had no answer to that. Better drop all such ruminations.

That October a young man from Emory began to date me. There was a strong physical attraction between us, and I began to wonder if I could be in love with Fred. But then one day I realized that there was neither spiritual nor intellectual rapport, or anything like oneness between us. I stopped dating Fred, tried to forget romance and concentrate on my studies.

But soon, inevitably, I was drawn back to Westminster Church and Peter because of an aching void in my life. This notation in my Journal is revealing:

> There are several reasons why I'm attracted to Peter. For one thing, he has so much poetry in his soul.
>
> There is such a kinship between poetry and religion. They both try to see into the heart of things.
>
> One of the reasons I could never fall in love with Fred is that he has no appreciation for the beautiful.
>
> But then added to that, Peter combines an inheritance of the best of the European tradition with an acquisition of the best of the American. He has such a capacity for affection and tenderness, such a luscious sense of humor sprinkled with an earthy roguishness.
>
> Why must the embodiment of all my ideal be 12 years older than I and as remote as the South Pole?

To my fellow students, I must have seemed on top of things. My grades were good, close to an "A" average. I had achieved success as an intercollegiate debater, in Poetry Club and in other class activities. Yet underneath it all, I was still churning:

> Tonight I feel compelled to write until my hand is tired and exhausted. I am restless and unhappy these days because I am neither right with myself nor with God. Why this dissatisfaction with myself? I am driven on and on by an overwhelming sense of some destiny, of some task to be done which I must do. I can never be peaceful and happy and enjoy life until I learn why I am here and where I am going.

It is as if my soul is frozen and hard, and when there comes some mellow influence which melts it, my soul strains against these walls like a turbulent mountain stream whose course has been newly freed from encumbering rubbish. And I don't think it too dramatic to say that my life is just as barren and dry as the rocky stream-bed, parched through being deprived of the life-giving water.

I am tired of knowing and not doing, tired of thinking and not being. I despise myself because I am simply lazy in my religion. It is easier not to bother. Yet I know that I can never find God by not bothering.

Throughout that winter and into the spring my Journal notes were peppered with references to Peter Marshall.

The more I hear him talk, the more I realize we have the same ideas and ideals—we like the same things... How I wish I could tell him all the sleep he has made me lose... Dreaming this way about Peter is the most foolish thing that has ever happened to me.

Reading through my journals of this period so many years later makes me aware as never before how tender God was with me, never intruding on my willful self-centeredness, but always there when the heart hungers inside me cried out. And how beautiful was his timing in the slow—agonizingly slow to me—way the relationship between Peter and me developed until I, so much younger, was mature enough to meet Peter where he was spiritually and intellectually.

The film version of *A Man Called Peter* indicated that the turning point in our relationship was May 3, 1935, the Prohibition Rally (turned into a Youth Rally in the movies) at which Peter and a student from Emory University and I spoke.

My Journal shows that this rally was an interesting but only an early step along the way. As we drove to the schoolhouse where the meeting was to take place, Peter focused his attention on me. Pointedly, he squelched the rumor that he was engaged by saying, "Don't believe everything you hear, my dear girl. I certainly am not even about to be married." He pronounced the word "mar-rr-ied" with a very broad "a" and a rolling of the "r's."

When the meeting began with the singing of some old revival hymns, Peter quickly entered into the spirit of the evening, his fine baritone voice ringing out above all others. One by one we were then elaborately introduced, listened to patiently, and given more applause than we deserved. Frankly, I can remember almost nothing about what we said.

On the return drive we were both in the back seat. Peter tucked his arm through mine and held my hand all the way home. He explained that he had been wanting to talk with me for a long time and had never before gotten a real chance. Before we said good-by Peter asked me if I ever went bowling and said that he would take me out some night.

Afterwards, I was ecstatic. My dream of two long years standing had at last been fulfilled—that of getting to know Peter better. I had never thought he would actually ask me for a date.

A week went by, then another, and still Peter did not call. There were two get-togethers at the church where he overflowed with warmth toward me. Each time he would go out of his way to drive me back to the college. On May 12 he asked to return for me at 3:30 that afternoon after which we were together until 11 o'clock that night—our first real date. Lingeringly, tenderly, he bade me goodnight, his last words, "I'll be in touch with you this week."

The days dragged by. No call. What was I to think?

When summer vacation came, I went home to West Virginia more frustrated than the year before. Why did he always seem so interested when I was with him, but then never followed up with a note or a telephone call?

He had promised to write—and did. The postmark on the letter was June 17, 1935. I tore it open eagerly. A typed letter was enfolded in a church bulletin. My face fell, my hopes plummeted as I read:

Dear Catherine:

Your card was most welcome. I am glad you thought of me. My summer's plans have now crystalized. I sail for Scotland from New York on July 5th and shall be gone until the end of August. They have given me a month's vacation and a month's leave of absence. I shall visit home and try to be with Mother more than I was last year. I'll be driving up to New York with a party of five others, which will make it rather difficult for me to detour and go through Keyser to see you as I had hoped.

Since you left I have been kept quite as busy as ever. I had only eight Commencements in eight days, but they almost wore me out before I got through. I have been at Agnes Scott all of last week, teaching in our Synodical Conference, and this week I preach every night at Villa Rica. I'll be melted away before I get to Scotland. Hope you are well, resting, and having a good time.

My best wishes and remembrances.

Peter

It could scarcely have been a more casual, impersonal letter! Disappointed again, once more I went through the summer process of trying to eliminate any thoughts of romance about Peter Marshall. In August came an even more casual card from Troon, Ayshire...

Having a grand time in Scotland. Spent a week in London and had so many fine trips. Hope you are having a fine summer. Regards,

Peter Marshall

That did it! It was time to stop acting like a schoolgirl and get on with the business of life.

Yet in thinking back over those few short here-and-there hours I had spent with him, I discovered that there were little things which had become memories dear to me: the peculiar look he had given me as we were standing by his car after his Mother's Day sermon when I told him how his idealism about women had moved me; the moment later that evening when his hand covered mine as we were leaning over the bridge and watching the moonlight as it made a patch of silver on the water; the intensity of his eyes looking into mine as we were driving out to Agnes Scott when he was telling me of his coming trip to Scotland; that moment when he came up behind me at the bowling alley and put his hands on my shoulders; later, the way he stroked my hair and said, "Little Catherine."

The ache in my heart continued though the summer and into the fall. I returned to college for my senior year determined to stay away from Westminster Church, convinced once and for all that there was no hope for the one thing my heart yearned for more than anything else. I must forget Peter Marshall.

Meanwhile, three years of college had greatly enriched and broadened the naïve, small-town girl from the West Virginia mountains. Whatever I lacked in ability I made up in heartfelt desire and intensity, and in hard, slugging work. In any discussion on world issues such as the League of Nations, Nazism, or America's economic collapse, my comments were never deliberate and measured but passionate, often laced with blazing indignation, prompting classmates to dub me "Calamity Catherine." Their inevitable joshing would finally bring me back to earth to find again some balance and the return of a sense of humor.

I must have averaged three hours a day in the college library where I dug into the classics, enjoyed novels, browsed poetry, dived into history, always enchanted with personalities, life style, and human interest data on

the men and women who had *made* history What delight
to happen one day upon Thomas Carlyle's precise expression of this approach: "History is the essence of innumerable biographies."

My reading ranged widely—from John Calvin's *Institutes*
to William Hazlitt's and Thomas Carlyle's *Essays*, to *The
Writings of James Madison*, to Dorothy Wordworth's *Journal*,
to Matthew Arnold's prose and poetry; I was fascinated
with published letters such as those of Horace Walpole
and John Keats, and with poets like Shelley, Wordsworth,
A.E. Housman; and I fell in love with Edna St. Vincent
Millay and Robert Frost, who visited our campus via the
lecture platform.

At the start of my senior year, I decided to pour all my
energies into my studies, debating, the Hiking Club and
Poetry Club. For a time I fancied myself the complete tragic
poet, wallowing in the shortness of life and equally gloomy
and too-serious subjects. Though it turned out that I was
never meant to be a poet, unwillingly I stumbled on an
important technique in learning to write. In poetry one
has to find the precise word. One's thoughts have to be
placed in small compass—sharp as an arrow. And imagination has to come into play, or the poetry is just blah or
worse—mushy.

Much of this effort was even in that demanding form,
the Shakespearean sonnet. There indeed was discipline—
ah, discipline! All of it fine training for writing.

My resolve to stay away from Westminster Church
lasted only until October 20 when I made this entry:

> Went to church at Westminster, but got there after
> 11 a.m. and had to sit in the vestibule and listen to
> Peter through the loud speaker. I had planned not to
> speak to him afterwards, but suddenly changed my
> mind. He pumped my hand and commented that this
> was the first time I had been here this year. So he *had*
> noticed my absence! He promised to get in touch with
> me. I shan't hold my breath until he does.

Gossip continues about the different women Peter goes out with. I don't think he plays around, but being a tender and affectionate person, succumbs for the moment and gives women the wrong impression. The reason he has never gotten married is that none of us has ever really come up to his ideal....

I was invited to have dinner with Peter at the Robinsons, to which he was quite late. Right away he brought up the past spring. Had I remembered it? We ended up looking at his pictures of Scotland, drinking tea, talking. He said he would call me, but I am skeptical. And so Peter once more invades my smug and fortified existence.

The entries in my journals for the next four months continued the pattern. When he saw me Peter was all interest. He arranged to take me to meals at a friend's where we talked, sang, played games like *Monopoly, Yacht, Parcheesi*. Once I was back on campus however, he seldom if ever called or sought me out. It's clear to me now that Peter as a bachelor in his early 30s and a preacher of growing importance was reluctant to take the initiative in seeking out dates with a college girl so many years younger than he. He knew that to others this would seem improper. And he was right. At the time I could not see this—or have any feel for God's timing in the situation.

The crucial turning point in our relationship came on Sunday, May 3, 1936. I had been asked to review a book at the Sunday afternoon fellowship hour at Peter's church. I chose one entitled *Prayer* by the Norwegian theologian, Dr. O. Hallesby, a professor at the Independent Theological Seminary of Oslo. This was an unusual book for any professor-theologian because its content was not theory; what Dr. Hallesby had to say seemed so obviously directly from his own experience.

Such an assignment would have been a challenge to me at any time and place. Since this was to be at Peter's church, and the pastor himself was likely to be in the audience, I did an inordinate amount of preparation. An intuition told me that this was the time and place for something important to happen between Peter and me—if it was ever meant to happen. The depths of Peter's inner being had been revealed to me through his preaching. But there had been no comparable chance for him to catch a glimpse of my inner spirit. The book review just might provide such a window into the real Catherine whom Peter had not yet seen. Hence the period of preparation for my talk was bathed in prayer. The writings of this Scandinavian seminary professor saturated my being.

When I arrived at the church that Sunday afternoon, the fellowship hall was filled with people, including Peter Marshall. Just before I was to speak I was stricken, almost paralyzed by tension and nervousness. Did I have anything really worthwhile to say to these knowledgeable people?

I felt so young and unimportant and unknowing. In my agony of self-doubt I closed my eyes and beseeched the Lord to rescue me, to place His hand on my trembling body, to calm my tumultuous thoughts so that words would come out which not only made sense, but would move these people toward a prayer life as the book had moved me.

"We tend to be superficial in our prayers," I began with quavering voice. "Most of us think of God as a kind of Santa Claus who waits to hear our requests. What He really wants to hear are the hungers of our heart and our confessions of deception and dishonesty."

Confidence and strength surged through my body. Since Dr. Hallesby had opened my eyes to my own smugness in certain areas, I admitted this and depicted how I had begun to change my approach to prayer. I confessed my hunger to know God better, to feel the Presence of Jesus, to be able to talk to Jesus as a Friend. I described situations like the Katherine Mansfield paper where I had felt so helpless in the face of the biting words of my English professor.

"The author has something to say about such situations which really helped," I said. Then I read this passage by Hallesby:

> Listen, my friend! Your helplessness is your best prayer. It calls from your heart to the heart of God with greater effect than all your uttered pleas. He hears it from the very moment that you are seized with helplessness, and He becomes actively engaged at once in hearing and answering the prayer of your helplessness. He hears today as He heard the helpless and wordless prayer of the man sick with the palsy.[1]

Because the book had revealed to me my own inadequacies, I confessed how self-righteous I had been during my college years. Emotion poured through my words as I described how the book had revitalized my prayer life. I felt lifted up and carried forward by a Power beyond myself.

Though the audience was quiet and attentive, it was Peter's face that commanded my attention. He stared at me with such an intentness that my stomach began churning. There was a moment when I almost felt that only the two of us were in the room.

After my talk Peter was subdued as he closed the meeting. He turned to me, took my hand and squeezed it tightly, a look in his blue-gray eyes I could not fathom. Then we went into the evening service where I made the mistake of sitting within three pews of the front.

My turbulent feelings and the emotion of the previous few hours were too much. The stone pillars and the Good Shepherd window behind the pulpit began to swim alarmingly. I was too sick to be embarrassed when Peter mentioned my name from the pulpit in connection with the talk I had just given. By the time he began his sermon, I knew it would be disastrous to stay.

As I rose to begin the longest walk in my life, the voice from the pulpit trailed off, and there was dead silence, broken only by the staccato clicking of my heels on the stone floor. I could feel Peter's eyes boring into my back every step of the way up the long aisle. Not until I was well out into the foyer did the voice resume over the loud speakers.

The college infirmary received me that night and attempted to diagnose this strange stomach ailment. The head nurse, properly starched and equipped with a strong nose for sniffing out lovesick maidens, had her suspicions.

The next day Peter and Ruby Coleman, his secretary, were eating lunch at Martha's Tea Room next door to the church. As a rule, they used that time to talk about church business or sermons. On this particular day, I learned later, Peter was unusually quiet. Ruby noticed that he seemed tense and introspective.

Suddenly he said, "You know, every time I meet a nice girl, she leaves town."

Ruby knew what he meant. She had been watching the slow unfolding of our friendship. She knew that in less than a month I would be graduating and leaving Atlanta.

"Well, look," she asked in her quiet way, "can't you do something about it?"

For a long moment Peter did not reply. He appeared to be in deep thought. Carefully, he buttered a roll. Then, "Maybe I can."

He did do something about it—within the next hour.

In the early afternoon the infirmary telephone at Agnes Scott rang, and the solicitous voice on the other end had a familiar Scottish accent.

"I'm talking from Miss Hopkins' office," the voice said. "I have secured her permission to come over and see you. May I?"

I gasped. No mere man—unless armed with a medical diploma—had ever, in all the college's history, been allowed inside the infirmary. Male visitors were simply taboo. After all, the young ladies were not properly clothed! How Peter had prevailed on Miss Hopkins I couldn't even imagine.

"I—really don't think you'd better," I said hastily. "I'm well enough to dress and come over. I'll meet you in the colonnade in ten minutes."

I should not have stopped him. Ever afterwards Peter accused me of having thwarted his only chance for fame with future generations of Agnes Scotters. If I had not interfered, as the first male visitor in this off-limits haven, Peter some day might have rated a bronze plaque on the infirmary wall in commemoration of the occasion.

Almost every day after that my Journal records items about the two of us.

> Peter was terribly solicitous about my illness... I believe now he wants to be serious... I think Peter is in love with me!!... Tonight we went to a play. Afterwards on the front porch he kissed me again and again... Tonight we talked until three in the morning and he proposed . . .

He framed his proposal in gentle words, like the delicate embroidery surrounding the strong, simple words of an old sampler.

And then a surprising thing happened to me. I found I could not give him an answer just then.

How strange! That made no sense. For three years I had been hopelessly in love with Peter Marshall (foolishly in love, I thought), and now had come the biggest moment of my life—a proposal from the man of my dreams. And I hesitated. Why?

It was because at that moment I became aware in a new way of how God operates in human lives, and in that moment of awareness, I did a lot of growing up. Suddenly I saw how wrong it is to go after what *we* want, and then—with considerable audacity—later ask God to bless it.

When Peter finally did propose, I wanted more than anything else to know God's will with certainty. Nothing else would do. The awareness of my ever-present will and emotions in this relationship was precisely why I could not now say "yes" without the sure knowledge that this marriage was not just my will, or even Peter's, but primarily God's will also.

When I shyly suggested to Peter that both of us needed to submit this decision to God in prayer, eagerly and quickly he agreed. So we prayed together, asking God if our fused lives and joint purposes would be a greater asset to the kingdom of God on earth than if we went our separate ways.

Almost from our first meeting I had had a strange sense of a God-given destiny about Peter. That made it of prime importance to be certain that I was meant to be a part of that destiny.

There followed days of praying about this separately. As unskilled and immature as I was in prayer, God chose this time to teach me a great lesson. I learned that because God loves us so much, He often guides us by planting His own lovely dream in the barren soil of a human heart. When the dream has matured, and the time for its fulfillment is ripe, to our astonishment and delight, we find that God's will has become our will, and our will, God's.

At the turning point of one of life's most important decisions, the choice of a life partner, Peter and I met God Himself. Only God could have thought of a plan like that!

As I took my last college examinations and wandered about the campus in something of a daze, a benediction slowly settled upon my head. What seemed too good to be true was true: God was not only giving His approval to this marriage, He had been in Peter's and my relationship all along, slowly guiding it and maturing it. In retrospect I could see that through all my impatience and frustration God had been the Divine Orchestrator of this romance in a way that would probably confound modern day romantics.

There remained only the pleasant task of giving Peter my answer.

I chose a moment when we were driving from Decatur to Atlanta.

"There's something I must tell you..." I began.

In the semi-darkness I could see a strained look cross Peter's face.

"Good... or bad?" he asked tensely.

When I then accepted his proposal of marriage, he said simply and fervently, "Thank the Lord!"

For several moments he drove along without saying anything more. When finally he stopped the car beside the road, it was to bow his head and to pray an achingly beautiful prayer. God was in every part of his life, he was God's, and with God he wanted to share this supreme moment. Only then did he take me into his arms.

On my graduation night Peter and I walked through an almost-deserted campus. I was to leave the next day.

The ancient oaks cast heavy shadows on the driveway, and the moon shone on white magnolia blossoms heavy with perfume. Main Hall had seen thousands of girls come and go. The venerable red-brick, ivy-covered walls had stood sentinel over many a tender farewell.

"If anybody had told me three months ago," said Peter, "that I would be standing in front of Main Hall telling the girl I love good-by and not caring whether all Decatur was at my back and all Atlanta at my front or who saw me, I would have thought they were crazy."

The night watchman, standing somewhere in the shadows, discreetly looked the other way.

The Marshall family

V

Illness

.....He maketh me
to lie down
in green pastures....

Psalm 23:2

Illness

Peter and I were married by my father in a simple church wedding on November 4, 1936 in Keyser, West Virginia. Later that same day my new husband and I traveled by train to Washington, D.C., and spent our honeymoon night at the Lee House Hotel. With considerable chagrin Peter had informed me several days before that he had agreed to meet the morning after the wedding with the pastoral committee of New York Avenue Presbyterian Church.

This prestigious old Washington church had literally grown up with the nation's capital. Located within two blocks of the White House, this was where Abraham Lincoln had attended midweek and Sunday services. The President had been scheduled to become a communicant member on April 19, 1865. But five days before, at a few minutes before ten at night, he was shot at close range, a bullet in his brain.

Ever the history enthusiast (with this subject as my major at Agnes Scott), I was awed by such historical ties and intimidated by the new role into which I was being so abruptly plunged. The morning after our marriage, Peter, still contrite about having to leave me alone in our bedroom at the Lee House Hotel, hastened out to meet the church committee already waiting for him in a room upstairs. "I'll telephone down when you're to come up, Catherine," were his parting words.

I dressed carefully, trying to calm my churning emotions. "Please, Lord," the terrified prayer went up, "don't let me embarrass Peter or fail him in any way."

The men and women of the committee, very kind to me and apologetic for interrupting our honeymoon, informed Peter, "We have hunted all over the country, and you are the man we want for the New York Avenue Church."

In the end, Peter turned down the call. There was still, he later wrote the committee, unfinished work for him in Atlanta. Nor did he feel ready for such a big assignment in Washington.

We settled into a cottage on Durand Drive in Atlanta which Peter, the romanticist, had himself selected during our engagement. The house with diamond-shaped, leaded windows sprawled over the top of a hill. The approach to our new home was by a rustic bridge over a brook winding its way around the base of the hill. Behind the house towered a grove of fragrant pine trees.

Having for a long time been a "boarder" in a friend's home, Peter's delight in having a home of his own knew no bounds. Enthusiastically he helped me select every item of furnishing (even in decorating he was not about to let any decision be a solely female one), and with equal zest planted spring bulbs all over the front hillside.

Yet the following year came a second call to the New York Avenue Church: "Since you turned us down, we have combed the country. You are *still* the man we want for this pastorate. Will you come?"

After much prayer, this time the answer had to be "yes." We had both learned during our courtship days that in relation to any specific prayer for guidance our preferences and wills have to be relinquished, laid on God's altar for Him to decide, before He will speak to us.

It was not Peter's personal preference to move to the nation's capital. He loved Atlanta. There he had found his footing, and the thought of leaving was agony. Yet our word was that God had some larger plan in the offing. Yes, we were to go.

So at only 23 the young girl who had fled up the back stairs to avoid involvement with people now had to be hostess to a steady stream of social functions in one of Washington's largest downtown churches. And our new home, the manse on Cathedral Avenue, was next door to "Woodley," the estate of Henry L. Stimson, soon to be Secretary of War.

Still in pursuit of excellence, I was all-out in my determination to succeed in this new role. Prayer for help brought exactly the needed friends to my side. Kind church women like Mrs. Frank Edgington and Isabella Stott filled me in on New York Avenue traditions established by the long string of pastors' wives before me dating back to 1803 and the Thomas Jefferson era. Friends outside the church such as Winifred Hanigan, with her know-how about clothing, took me firmly in hand. I could no longer look like a small-town girl lately come to the big city. Anita Ritter, the mistress of an impressive town house on Massachusetts Avenue, gave me a crash course on Washington protocol, the do's and don'ts of the social and political scene. Soon the intensity of my efforts on all fronts was pushing me past my physical boundaries.

On the snowy Sunday morning of January 21, 1940 I bore my husband a son. Shortly before nine that morning the obstetrician gave Peter and my mother the news, "Congratulations, Dr. Marshall. It's a boy—a fine son."

The new father was ecstatic, almost awestruck. "A *son!* We have a son! How wonderful!"

What to name him? My husband wanted to keep the "Peter" since this had already been in the Marshall family for two generations. Finally, it was decided: the baby's name would be Peter John.

Now our happiness was complete.

Peter had often commented that trouble sends us no telegraphed warnings. So we discovered. Three years after Peter John's birth, I was to find out that even our greatest human desire and all-out effort are never enough.

Suddenly illness struck me down. Having almost fainted at a church meeting, I went to *Johns Hopkins* in Baltimore for a complete physical check-up.

After days of tests and X-rays, Dr. Thomas Sprunt's summary of my medical situation was devastating. The diagnosis was tuberculosis, with me ordered to bed full time. "Since tests have uncovered no infection-spreading bacilli," the doctor explained, "you can stay at home. But you should not, must not, do any housework or, in fact, work of any kind."

"But—but I can't go to bed," I stammered out. "I have a three-year-old son. He needs me."

"Mrs. Marshall," the voice was stern, "total bed rest is mandatory. You have no choice. There is no other cure. Just consider yourself fortunate that it's not a sanitarium."

"Then how long do you think it will take me to get well?" My voice was now almost a whisper.

Dr. Sprunt hesitated a long moment. "Oh, possibly three or four months." Then seeing my stricken face, "Mrs. Marshall, don't feel so badly about it. People *do* recover from tuberculosis."

When I later rushed sobbing into Peter's arms to blurt out the news, he was as stunned as I. For once, this most articulate of men was without words and mutely tried to comfort me with touch and caresses.

Dr. Sprunt turned my case over to a Washington lung specialist. A trained nurse was necessary because I was not allowed even to feed myself. Any arm motion might interfere with healing of the chest. Miss Mildred Beall, an RN from our church, volunteered for the emergency.

The specialist's orders: between-meal eggnogs to put weight on me; temperature to be taken six times a day and recorded; one chest X-ray per month; I could get out of bed only to go to the nearby bathroom.

But who would take care of Peter John? And how would any of us explain what was happening to a desolate three-year-old who needed his mother?

Our son was given a tuberculin skin test. Results: negative. So he was allowed to trot in and out of the bedroom. Years later, an indelible picture rises to meet me... Peter John, tall for his age at three, standing with his back to one of the windows, the light behind him making an aureole of his blond curls, staring at me lying there flat in bed, his big round blue eyes sad, hurt, and questioning.

It took all the will power I had to keep from jumping out of bed and running to him to hug him close.

There was no way. There stood the nurse watchfully, with sympathetic eyes.

"You can sit on the bed, and I'll tell you a story," I told Peter John limply. "Maybe later on we can play games together."

Sorry substitutes. I knew full well that such makeshift gestures could not provide the security our son needed. My mother came to take care of him and stayed as long as she could. There followed a long string of maids, nurse-maids and assorted government girls. Help of any kind was very scarce, for we were now two years into World War II.

And so one interminable month dragged by after another.

On an especially low day Peter would often stand in the bedroom looking down at me propped up on the pillows, and turn prophet. "Cath'rine, someday you will look back with gratitude on these bleak days as some of the richest of your life." Then, seeing my incredulous inability to receive his words: "Besides, Cath'rine, you know perfectly well, *all* discouragement is of Satan."

I just wanted to throw a book at my Scottish prophet. Whereupon he would grin and pat my cheek and kiss me, turn on his heel and depart for the church office.

Yet looking back, I know that Peter was right. For me those two years in bed were a continuation in depth of the voyage of self-discovery and God-discovery begun in college.

The unforgettable truth of David's Psalm 23 came alive in my experience: "He *maketh* me to lie down in green pastures..." thus sometimes using illness to get our full attention. For me this became a period of equipping—of spiritual preparation—for a tumultuous life of changes, of great, high moments to follow and plunging low points. From the vantage point of the years, I can see now that my being forced to lie down in the green pastures beside very still waters indeed—the isolation of our bedroom— was a time of training. Day by day God was the Teacher and I, the pupil.

I was led through four areas of instruction in the "Green Pasture" classroom. The first had to do with becoming personally acquainted with my Lord, His character, His personality, and how He deals with us humans. And my first assignment in achieving that objective was a big one. I was to read and become knowledgeable about His Book in a new way. For Scripture is the ongoing story of how He has dealt with other men and women living through every conceivable experience; further, in it we discover what His will is for us humans and what it is not.

But there was more to this new way (new for me) of reading Scripture. I was to expect Jesus Himself to speak to me through the messages of His Book as I lay so helpless in bed, then to go further and also communicate to me through the "still, small Voice" in my spirit. After only a few days of this, I felt the necessity of writing down in my Journal the thoughts and insights He was giving.

One of my initial, joyous discoveries about Jesus' will is that having Himself created these awesomely constructed bodies of ours, of *course* He wants us to be well. All over the gospels is Jesus' positive zest for healing the diseased or the handicapped or the blind. In fact, he drew vicious criticism from the religious authorities because He could not wait even 24 hours to heal certain sufferers, thus unabashedly proceeding to break the Jewish Sabbath law, since in Jewish law, healing was "work."

And Scripture makes it plain that Jesus is "the same yesterday, today, and forever," projecting into future ages the same power He had while on earth in the flesh, and specifically passing on that power to future disciples who accept His full Lordship.

Then I had to conclude that my father and many another preacher had been mistaken. For in so many of their seminaries they had been taught that the gospel miracles were extended into the first century for a short time just to get the Church started and were never meant for now or for any future dispensation.

Since this very different message from Scripture was living water for my thirsty spirit and needy body, I received it with overwhelming eagerness. As I shared every bit of it with Peter, he himself dived into the subject of Christian healing. Soon it was spilling over into a series of sermons on this subject.

But then with the over-simplified presumption of the

typical new pupil, I expected Peter's and my joint prayers for my healing to bring quick results.

Not only that, enthusiastically I shared this wonderful discovery with other sufferers. Kenneth Gray, the Scottish groundskeeper on the Stimson estate next door, was dying of a brain tumor. And we had just received word that Gertrude, a dear woman in our church, was also dangerously ill with cancer. Surely, they too could claim for themselves those wondrous promises all through the Bible:

.... I will put none of those diseases upon thee, which I have brought upon the Egyptians: for *I am the Lord that healeth thee* (italics added).[1]

Surely he (Jesus on His Cross) *hath* borne our griefs and carried our sorrows.... and with his stripes we are healed.[2]

Is any sick among you? let him call for the elders of the church; and let them pray over him, anointing him with oil in the name of the Lord: And the prayer of faith shall save the sick, and the Lord shall raise him up[3]...

And had not God promised us that His word "would *never* return unto Him void"?[4] Then surely our claiming with faith any one of these promises for ourselves was the way to healing.

Yet it did not work the way I expected. As test after test followed, my high sedimentation rate was not coming down, and the chest X-rays remained unchanged.

Still I had gained weight, and the trained nurse had long since departed. By June, 1944 I could be up for several periods each day of thirty minutes or so. I would help Peter John dress for school and sometimes eat dinner with the family at night.

But Dr. Sprunt had said three or four months; this was not much progress for fourteen months. What was wrong?

How had I misinterpreted? My Teacher had yet to show me the difference between the presumption that masquerades as faith and real faith. The dividing line between the two lies at the point of one's motive.

When eventually both cancer victims died, I was shown that without realizing it, I had fallen into the trap of presumption in praying for Kenneth Gray and Gertrude Wiber. In effect, like this: "Here's Your Word about healing, Lord, right here. You said it. I believe it and claim it in faith. Now You prove it by doing it."

Later on the truth hit me: Our sovereign, omnipotent God has no need to "prove" anything to any one of us, His creatures. Who are we to ask for *that!*

Then I realized that Jesus' third wilderness temptation had been precisely this one—to substitute presumption for faith. For Satan had led Him into Jerusalem to the highest pinnacle of the temple, and there had taunted Him:

> .... If thou be the Son of God, cast thyself down from hence....[5]

Whereupon Satan, himself knowing Scripture very well, went on to quote one of God's rich promises about angelic protection.

> .... He shall give his angels charge over thee, to keep thee....[6]

Instantly Jesus resisted with the rebuke:

> Thou shalt not tempt the Lord thy God.[7]

Then what *was* the way to real faith? Subsequently I would be shown the difference between the *logos,* one of the two Greek nouns used for God's written word in Scripture, and the *rhēma.* The latter is that part of the logos to which the Holy Spirit points us personally, which He illuminates and brings to life for us in our particular situation.

For instance, out of all the Old Testament *logos*, the Spirit had pointed out to me and emblazoned into my consciousness, nine words from the second verse of Psalm 23: *He maketh me to lie down in green pastures.* Those nine words were His rhēma spoken directly by the Lord Himself to me.

The point is that Jesus will not allow us to use Scripture as only an historical document or as a set of automatic rules. To do so is to ignore the risen, living Lord standing there just beside us at any given moment, as He promised He would, as well as the Holy Spirit in us to interpret, teach and to guide us into Truth (John 16:13). So our Lord stands sentinel over His Book to show us that we can use His word in Scripture with real power only as He Himself energizes it and speaks to us personally through it.

Was not this precisely what He was teaching us when He said,

> You search the scriptures, because you think that in them you have eternal life; and it is they that bear witness to me; *yet you refuse to come to me* that you may have life (italics added).[8]

We cannot do without our study of the logos, for that will ever be the treasure-pool out of which the rhēma is lifted. But only the rhēma has the power-thrust to cope with Satan's onslaught on our spirits, relationships or bodies.

It was increasingly obvious that my courses in the green pastures classroom had scarcely begun.

Gently, the Lord then led me to the second area of instruction: honesty and complete openness and transparency before Him. He is always Light, so I too must walk in the light. All closet doors, every shuttered room in me must be thrown open. So began months of soul searching. *One Journal entry was deeply revealing.*

> This morning came a disturbing thought. For years I have yearned for a free time away from household duties for a quiet time—alone, undisturbed. I was never able to obtain it—until I went to bed sick last March. *Could I have wanted to be rid of the burdens of daily living so much that I had a deep unconscious desire for illness as an escape—once I had made the difficult adjustment to bed rest—from them?* In this sense therefore, my illness has been satisfying. I have had all the time I wanted for quiet communication with the Lord, and others have carried my burdens for me.
>
> The Lord has asked me the direct question, "Do you really want to be well?" In other words, "Are you ready to face up to life, to assume the responsibilites of a normal person?"
>
> I can see that He wants me to be well. He wants to cure me. He wants my answer to be "yes." Therefore, to say "no" would be to frustrate His will.
>
> One part of me wants to be well, but another part of me is still hugging the bed, still exceedingly loath to part with it. I have given Him my will in the matter though, and asked Him to heal this schism in me, to make me want His will totally and to give me joy in it.

Disturbing thoughts! Pondering them, I even sensed that there was significance in the fact that one symptom of my lung disease was breathlessness: ever since moving to Washington I had been literally panting to carry the load I had insisted upon assuming.

Of course from the very beginning of my illness, Peter and I had regularly prayed together for my healing. Thus it was a shock to discover that a split-off part of me could have been voiding these prayers.

What else did I need to uncover so that a healing could take place?

I knew that anything unloving in me, any resentment, unforgiveness or impurity would shut out God, just as a muddy windowpane obscures the sunlight. Painfully, in agony of mind and spirit, I began thinking back over my life, recalling all too vividly all my transgressions and omissions.

There grew in me a desire for total honesty, born of desperation. I began to see that my wholeness was more than the search for physical health. That would come only as inner cleavages were healed, as I was more closely joined to the Source of my being.

In my prayer time I stood before my Maker starkly, stripped of pretenses. My unworthiness shrieked at me. My tendency to overcriticalness, to harsh, hasty judgments. My little jealousies, the self-centeredness that had made me a poor one for teamwork of any kind.

Lying in bed I summoned up the dishonesties of my past. Once in high school I had cheated on an algebra test. Another time when I had been treasurer of a school organization, I had "borrowed" some money from the fund and then paid it back ten days later.

There were dishonesties of a different sort: I had not always been candid with my husband. That same secretiveness I had been aware of as a little girl had surfaced in marriage as a tendency to bar Peter from a corner of my mind and heart. I well knew that this was no way to build a solid marriage.

Through agonizing days I made methodical notes on these ignoble traits and deeds. Then I asked Peter to hear me out on the ones that affected him. He listened, looking pained, not so much at what I was confessing as at the spiritual anguish he saw in me.

Surely now I had done all that was needed to receive a healing. My prayer went like this, "Lord, I have asked You to cleanse me of the dark spots in my life. I claim Your healing right now for my lungs. I ask that this healing be shown on the next tests.'

Eagerly I sought new tests. They were made and the report came back: no change in my lung condition.

Despair settled in. My prayers must still be inadequate. After more than a year in bed, where was I? My husband and four-year-old son needed me more than ever. As I tried to supervise the running of our home from my bed, our household situation was becoming more difficult with every month that passed.

The summer of 1944 came, and we went to our Cape Cod cottage for two and a half months. I got there through the special arrangements of a compartment on the train and an ambulance to meet me at the station.

At the Cape the Lord led me into the third phase of His teaching. First, I had made progress in getting to know Him better. Second, being ruthlessly honest about myself had given me an openness to receive more of His love and riches. Then one morning I found myself with a sudden and intense interest in the Holy Spirit. Questions nagged and would not be silenced. What was so significant about this ghostly-sounding term? Why had the Church clung tenaciously to something seemingly so archaic? In short, what was this Holy Spirit all about?

Obviously, God Himself had carefully planted the curiosity in me, for it was no passing whim. It did not go away, and it had ample emotional, intellectual, and volitional energy fueling it to keep me at a summer-long quest for answers to my questions.

I decided to go to the one place I could count on for final authoritative truth—the Bible. Scripture had never yet deceived me or led me astray. From long experience I knew that the well-worn words from the Westminster Shorter Catechism which I had memorized as a child in Missis-

sippi, had it exactly right: the Bible still is "the only infal-
lible rule of faith and practice."

At the same time I also knew that the search in Scripture
could be no random dipping in; it had to be thorough and
all-inclusive. A Bible, a Cruden's *Concordance*, a loose-leaf
notebook, pen and colored pencils were essential tools.

All summer I gave a minimum of an hour a day to this.
Using the various terms referring to the third Person of
the Trinity, I looked up every reference in the concordance,
Old and New Testament. Morning by morning revealed
new truths—new to me at least. Such as that in Old Testament times only certain prophets, priests, and kings
were given the Spirit. Even then, the Spirit was given them
only "by measure"—that is, a partial giving. So that was
why Joel's prophecy, fulfilled at Pentecost, was such startling news: in that great day the Spirit for the first time in
history became available to *all* flesh, no longer "by measure" but in His fullness![9]

The messages kept piling up. Though not a one of us
can recognize Jesus as who He really is until the Spirit
reveals this to us, nonetheless the *fullness* of the Holy Spirit
is *not* something that happens automatically at conversion.
His coming to us and living within us is a gift, the best
gift the Father can give us. But the Father always waits on
our volition. Jesus told us that we have to desire this gift
of gifts, ask for it—ask for Him.

Something else shimmered through too. It's the Spirit
who is the Miracle-Worker. When our churches ignore
Him, no wonder they are so devoid of answered prayer.
No wonder they have rationalized and developed an un-
scriptural position: the belief that miracles were only for
the beginning years of the faith to get the Church started!

Rather, the truth is that Scripture assumes miracles. And
the Helper (one of the names Jesus gave the Holy Spirit)
always brings miracles in His wake, moves in the climate
of the miraculous, not antithetical to "natural" law, simply
superseding it.

By now I was excited. I was also increasingly incredulous about the silence of the churches on this subject. How was it that I could not recall ever hearing a sermon on the Holy Spirit? Why was this not taught in Sunday School?

As the summer wore on I got out of bed more and more for brief periods. One morning I stood at the bedroom window looking out at the garden Peter had so lovingly planted... roses and white hollyhocks, yellow day-lilies, zinnias, all a riot of color... A blue sky above, the sea just over the brow of the hill.

Suddenly I knew that He was calling me to a new step of faith. The subject of obedience was to be the fourth stage of my training. It was a natural follow-up to what I had been learning about His nature, about honesty and about the Holy Spirit. I took a deep breath.

"Lord, from this moment I promise that I'll try to do whatever You tell me in order to get well, insofar as You'll make clear to me what Your wishes are. I'm weak, and many times I'll probably want to renege on this. But Lord, You'll have to help me with that, too."

I was trembling. I knew that this was a more all-out commitment to the Lord than that initial step at age nine when my father had given an altar call, and I had gone forward.

Yet nothing seemed different. The hollyhock faces still nodded at the window. Fluffy clouds still floated in the blue, blue sky. I turned and noted in my journal the date and the hour of the promise I had just made. There would be moments in the future when this pledge would not seem real to me. But it was real, and writing it down would help to remind me.

The proof of the reality of the pledge I had made began coming in the weeks that followed. My physical condition *was* improving. Each morning I would lie in the yard, soaking up sunshine. Next I began regularly joining the family for dinner. Then I began taking short walks some afternoons with Jeffrey, our cocker spaniel, trotting beside me.

It was a joy to stand at the top of the rise in the road and see the sea again, feel the tangy salt air on my cheeks, laugh at the sea wind blowing back Jeffrey's floppy ears as he stood poised, watching the circling gulls. It was even good to feel sand in my shoes.

But this stage too began with a setback. The many months of invalidism had eroded my self-worth as a mother and wife. My son needed me, but I still could not romp with him in the yard, or run with him along the beach, or go for long walks with him to hunt for shells, or to pick blueberries or beachplums. Peter John loved the out-of-doors, and I had to stay mostly inside. In the evenings I could read to him, but I could tell that he was becoming a lonely, wistful child, especially when his father had to be away for preaching or speaking engagements.

My husband was always understanding, loving, sympathetic, but he too resented my confinement indoors. When I heard his throaty, infectious laugh as he visited with the neighbors next door or quickly separated his Scottish brogue from other voices in a neighborhood discussion, my heart ached, and then I would have to battle self-pity.

At this point the imp with the pitchfork could wedge into my thoughts. *Peter is bored with you. He is tired of waiting on you. He likes healthy people around him. Fascinating women are always attracted to him.*

My Journal had this notation:

> There is fear in me that someone else will usurp my place in Peter's heart. I have often tried to make myself believe that it is fear for Peter, his reputation, his ministry and his spiritual welfare. But is it really? Isn't it simply fear for myself? I have prayed about this over and over and get temporary peace, but then soon the

same old fears engulf me again. Today I prayed that God would show me *how* to pray about it, that He would show me the lever by which I could lift it up to Him.

Within a matter of minutes this verse clearly came to me: "Resist not evil." In other words, the way to win out when I feel evil at work in my life and the lives of those I love is not to fight it in the ordinary sense, but to give over those I love completely into the Father's hands, knowing that I am helpless to cope with evil, but that "He is able."

I am to let my loved ones walk on into the lion's den; let evil come on in any guise it chooses—God will shut the lions' mouths. God will surround the one given over to Him with a league of His angels. If I think no evil thoughts, God will not let me be hurt, because I am willing to trust him.

This answer was of enormous help to me. Then in the days that followed God gave me further instructions:

Don't let your whole horizon be filled with Peter. Invite Mac and Polly for games some night.

I did as instructed. It was an evening of fun which Peter thoroughly enjoyed. The next instruction was even more surprising:

Get a new robe—a pretty feminine one.

Peter went with me to help me pick it out. Eagerly, I awaited the next message. It was in the same light vein:

Take an interest in the house again. Try doing your part to make it a home—not just a sleeping place.

As of old I began taking an interest in the garden and kitchen, surprised that strength somehow came to do each little task. I arranged flowers each day for the house. I asked members of the household to gather beach plums so that I could make jelly.

The summer ended, and our family had to return to Washington. With new confidence I went for the usual X-ray check-up of my lungs, only to get the report: "No perceptible change."

And I had thought that I was well on my way out of this morass of illness! Now I plummeted into real despair.

At this new crisis-point Peter John and I went to the eastern shore of Virginia to spend two weeks with my parents who were then living at Seaview. There I tried to reassess the lengthy road I had traveled. For two years I had given my all to learn of the Lord and to try to obey Him. Seemingly, I had tried everything, followed every lead, gone down every path. Yet here I was, still in bed for most of every day.

Only one way was left. Perhaps I had held back one heart's desire. So after many days of struggling, I handed over to God every last vestige of self-will, even my intense desire for complete health. Finally I was able to pray, "Lord, I understand no part of this, but if You want me to be an invalid for the rest of my life—well, it's up to You. I place myself in Your hands, for better or for worse. I ask only to serve You."

In the middle of that night I was awakened. The room was in total darkness. Instantly sensing something alive, electric in the room, I sat bolt upright in bed. Past all credible belief, suddenly, unaccountably, Christ was there, in Person, standing by the right side of my bed. I could see nothing but a deep, velvety blackness around me, but the bedroom was filled with an intensity of power, as if the Dynamo of the universe were there. Every nerve in my body tingled with it, as with a shock of electricity. I knew that Jesus was smiling at me tenderly, lovingly, whimsically—as though a trifle amused at my too-intense seriousness about myself. His attitude seemed to say, "Relax! There's not a thing wrong here that I can't take care of."

His personality held an amazing meld I had never before met in any one person: warm-hearted compassion and the light touch, yet unmistakable authority and kingliness. Instantly, my heart wanted to bow before Him in abject adoration.

Would He speak to me? I waited in awe for Him to say something momentous, to give me my marching orders.

"Go," He said in reply to my unspoken question, "Go, and tell your mother. That's easy enough, isn't it?"

I faltered, thoughts flicking through my mind. "Tell her"—*what* exactly? Jesus' words had an enigmatic quality.

Then came the next thought. *What will Mother think? It's the middle of the night. She'll think I've suddenly gone crazy.*

Jesus said nothing more. He had told me what to do. At that moment I understood as never before the totality of His respect for the free will He has given us and the fact that He will *never* violate it. His attitude said, "The decision is entirely yours."

But I also learned at that moment the life-and-death importance of obedience. There was the feeling that my future hung on my decision. So brushing aside any inconsequential thoughts of Mother's reaction, with resolution I told Him, "I'll do it if it kills me"—and swung my legs over the side of the bed.

How was it that though I could "see" nothing with the retina of my own eyes, I was yet aware of the gentle humor in His eyes as He quietly stood aside to let me pass?

I groped my way into the dark hall to the bedroom directly across from mine and spoke softly to Mother and Dad. Startled, Mother sat bolt upright in bed. "Catherine, is anything wrong? What—what on earth has happened?"

"It's all right," I reassured them. "I just want to tell you that I'll be all right now. It seemed important to tell you tonight. I'll give you the details tomorrow."

When I returned to the bedroom, that vivid Presence was gone. I found myself more excited than I have ever been before or since and more wide awake. It was not until the first streaks of dawn appeared in the eastern sky that I slept again.

The next day that extraordinary visitation was as vivid as it had been during the night hours. Yet there remained the ambiguity of the message I had been told to give Mother. Had Jesus meant that I was as of now totally healed? Or could this be a modern example of the way He had steadily used in the Biblical accounts, "according to your faith be it unto you?"

After breakfast I related the complete story to my parents. Next I wrote Peter a long letter describing every detail of this experience. Peter was never a letter-saver. Yet years later after his death, I found my letter written that day carefully stored among his important papers.

After my return to Washington, we awaited the next chest X-rays with special eagerness. For the first time there was marked improvement. And from then on, steady progress. In six months the doctors pronounced me completely well.

The years bring ever-fresh insights to what remains to this day the most real and vivid experience of my life. For it appeared that Jesus had not come to give an instantaneous healing, but to continue His teaching. There was also the total assurance that He loved me and had been with me all the way.

That night also gave me an understanding of Jesus' resurrection body and of the spiritual bodies we shall have after death. For in the bedroom at Seaview there was no vision as seen with the retinas of my eyes, no voice as heard with my human eardrums. No such crude equipment was needed to "see" Him, to "hear" every word He spoke, to catch every nuance of that compellingly vivid Personality.

Just so shall it be in the next life. Our spiritual bodies will have every faculty of our earthly tabernacles, only with heightened sensitivity and wonderful new freedom. We shall remember and know ourselves to be ourselves and recognize each other. We shall bask in His joyous, loving, delightful companionship.

Most important of all, He had shown me through more than two years of illness that I would always need Him every day for the rest of my life and more, throughout eternity.

At last I had the answer to my child's question about "enjoying Him forever!"

VI

Grief

....and whoever lives
and believes in Me
shall never die.
Do you believe this?

John 11:26—RSV

Grief

$\approx$

At 8:25 that morning the telephone rang. It was a call from the George Washington University Hospital with the message that my husband had died of a heart attack a few minutes before. My mind could not comprehend it. How could *Peter* be dead? Surely God would somehow yet intervene.

"Don't move him. Don't touch him until I get there," was my instinctive reply.

After I arrived at the hospital, the young doctor who walked with me to the door of Peter's room was solicitous. His eyes searching my face, he asked quietly, "Are you *sure* you want to go in there alone?"

"Oh, *yes*," I told him.

Saying nothing more, he withdrew.

As I opened the door and stepped inside the small room, there was the instantaneous awareness that I was not alone. Yet the man I loved was not in the still form on the bed. Though I did not understand it then and cannot explain it now, I knew that Peter was near and alive. And beside him was another Presence of transcendent glory, the Lord he had served through long years—years stretching back to his young manhood in Scotland.

Having already experienced that glory, how could I ever again doubt the fact of immortality? In a deep and intuitive way, beyond argument or intellectual process, deeper than tears, transcending words, came the knowledge that human life does not end in six feet of earth.

Yet the realization of the splendor was not to last. In that still hospital room, at a precise moment, the two vivid presences withdrew. Suddenly I saw Death stripped bare, in all its ugliness. With very human eyes I saw it: the fact of the man so dear to me. *There's nothing pretty about death. Those who sentimentalize it, lie. Carbon dioxide escaping from the sagging jaw. The limp hands. The coldness and white, white pallor of the flesh.*

Shivering, I rose to leave the room. I knew that this would be the last time on this earth that I would look upon my husband's face. So there in the hospital room, I said my last *au revoir*.

Now there was nothing to do but walk out. I sensed that out beyond the door, out beyond the chilly hospital corridor, a new life awaited me. That was the last thing in the world I wanted. But then Peter had not wanted a new life either—not yet anyway—not at just 46. And already he was embarked on that other adventure.

Two paces from the door, I was stopped as by an invisible hand. As I paused, a message was spoken with emphasis and clarity, not audibly, but with that peculiar authority I had come to recognize as the Lord's own voice: *Surely, goodness and mercy shall follow you all the days of your life.*

It was His personal pledge to me and to a son who would now sorely miss his father.

Looking back, I could see that God had been preparing

me for the shock of Peter's death during my two-year illness. The "green pastures" classroom had taught me my helplessness and the how of depending on Him as my only strength and resource.

During the funeral preparations and all the myriad decisions to be made, it was as though I were taken over and managed. In addition, a sort of protective shield was placed over my emotions. Somehow for those days I was lifted into a higher realm. Was *this*, I wondered, what it felt like actually to be living in the kingdom of God on earth?

The series of detailed instructions that issued from my mouth were straight from Him. The seeming maturity I was showing to Peter John, to my family, and to the members of our grieving congregation was the gift of His pure grace.

Then about eight days after Peter's death, suddenly that higher realm in which I had been so lovingly enveloped was gone, and I plummeted to earth to stand again on feet of clay in the valley where salt tears and loneliness and the fear of coping alone with the problems of everyday life are all too real.

My Lord was nearby of course, ready to help me all the way. Yet I sensed that another painful but necessary growth process stretched ahead.

At this point, the first need of the bereaved person is for comfort. God has pledged us that as part of our rightful inheritance as children of the King:

> For thus saith the Lord... As one whom his mother comforteth, so will I comfort you....[1]

This comfort had certainly been given me in the hospital room just after Peter's death. And it had continued during the days of shock and numbness right afterwards, granted,

I'm sure, by a loving Father who recognized my desperate need of knowing that He had not deserted me.

Then I found that some of the loveliest words of Scripture are for the longer-term soreness of heart that follows:

> I will not leave you comfortless....[2]

> ... he hath sent me to bind up the brokenhearted... to appoint unto them that mourn in Zion, to give unto them beauty for ashes, the oil of joy for mourning, the garment of praise for the spirit of heaviness...[3]

I was surprised to find that a great number of promises in the Bible are directed specifically to widows and to children who have had to part with one or both parents:

> The Lord will destroy the house of the proud; but he will establish the border of the widow.[4]

> Yet leave to me your orphans, I will save them; let your widows trust to me.[5]

And some of the most beautiful assurances of all are contained in that extraordinary 54th chapter of Isaiah addressed to us women, a chapter to be read over and over in its entirety by the deserted or bereaved until absorbed into one's bloodstream:

> Fear not . . . (thou) shalt not remember the reproach of thy widowhood any more . . . For the Lord hath called thee as a woman forsaken and grieved in spirit . . . with great mercies will I gather thee....

> And all thy children shall be taught of the Lord; and great shall be the peace of thy children.[6]

Yet there is another side to God's comfort for His ways are never man's ways. His is not the feather-cushion kind or a pat on the cheek, "There, there, dear child." It does not tiptoe into the chamber of grief with its shuttered windows: it marches in. There is steel at its backbone. It is a bugle call for reinforcements. It makes us remember that the word "comfort" is derived from the word *fortis*—which means "strength" or "strong."

God comforts us with strength by adding resources. His way is not to whittle down the problem but to build up our ability to cope with it...

> Fear not; (there is nothing to fear) for I am with you; do not look around you in terror and be dismayed, for I am your God. I will strengthen you and harden you (to difficulties); yes, I will help you; yes, I will hold you up and retain you with My victorious right hand of rightness and justice."[7]

It should not surprise us that a mainstay of God's comfort-resources are His people, the fellowship of believers. In the healing of my grief a first important step He asked me to take was to open my heart wide to other people.

When a deep injury to the spirit has been sustained—and grief *is* a real wound in the spirit and the emotions—the tendency of the sorrowing is to shut the heart and bar the door lest hurt be heaped upon hurt. Therefore, His insistence that we not give in to this will seem stringent indeed at the time.

When my own private crisis came, certainly I knew nothing about the way out of grief. I had never heard that psychologists and psychiatrists consider the matter of establishing new patterns of interaction with other human beings one of the most important laws for recovery. Or that from the standpoint of the experienced Christian counselor, the sorrowing one who almost involuntarily shuts his heart against his friends and lets bitterness creep in is, in a tragic way, insulating himself against that re-energizing love of God.

Part of the miracle of God's direction to me was His enabling me immediately after my husband's death to open my heart wider than ever before. I knew that it had to be God's doing because something broke through that deep reserve and thirst for privacy I had known since childhood.

The Sunday after Peter's death I was able to return to the New York Avenue Church and to sit with Peter John in our usual place in the pastor's pew. It would be excruciatingly hard, that I knew. For it would dramatize for me as nothing else could the fact that Peter Marshall would never again stand in that pulpit.

At points in the service I was unable to stop the flow of tears. Yet somehow, in thus facing reality, they became healing tears. God granted me the immediate gift of a warm-hearted Chinese woman who reached out to cover my hand with hers. I knew that she was sitting there ministering to me through prayer during the entire service.

The next day one couple who had been particularly fond of Peter came by the manse and sought me out in my bedroom. I remember that the young wife, her cheeks wet with tears, threw her arms around my neck. "Darling," she cried, "I love you so. We're going to have to stick awfully close together now."

My split-second choice at that moment was made by instinct—not in my conscious mind at all. It was a choice of whether or not I would merely politely tolerate such an overflowing exuberance of love—or really accept it. In yielding to it, I found a oneness with all human beings, a kinship with all suffering in the world—an authentic glimpse of the kingdom of God actually at work in a given community.

And so I opened wide the door of the manse. People came with warm handclasps and tear-filled eyes. They brought what they knew best how to make—soup, chicken salad, baked ham, angel food cake, custard, chess pie. The love that flowed like a great tidal wave through the Christian community of our church family blessed us all.

Those who helped me most were the few who understood about the stringent side of God's way of comforting and avoided the soft and gentle commiserating words which carry the unspoken message, "I feel sorry for you." Our response to that is usually self-pity. And self-pity is one of the worst of all stumbling blocks to the healing of grief.

Understanding what deadly poison the "poor-me" attitude is, how much I have come to value those tough-minded friends who dealt with me incisively when I was ill or grief-stricken.

One such friend was Anita, a tall, stately woman with the gift of rare discernment. I recalled one occasion during my illness when she had come to the manse to call.

On this particular afternoon, Anita had not walked into my bedroom—she had marched in. She had not even bothered to sit down.

Standing in the middle of the big room, she had cleared her throat as for a speech. Her eyes were sparking as much light as the star sapphire on her right hand. "Catherine, you've been on my mind for days. I've been tempted to feel sorry for you. Well, I'll be damned if I'll feel sorry for you. Forgive the language, but I feel just that vehemently about it.

"Pity wouldn't help you a bit. Besides, why should I pity you? You have all you need—the strength and guidance of God Himself."

Her words had been flung at me like ice water striking my face. I might have resented them, but I had not. In fact, when I had recovered from the first shock of the ice water, I had felt exhilarated, even as Anita had hoped I would.

Enough of this weakness and secluded life, had been my immediate reaction. *I'm going to get out of here.* And courage and the will to fight weakness and disease had mounted in me like mercury rising in a thermometer in the sun.

That day Anita had taught me an unforgettable lesson about the efficacy of following God's way in seeking to comfort one another. During those years, I had had hundreds of sickroom calls. Yet that one visit of Anita's towered like a mountain top above the others. Even remembering it helped because this was the kind of friend I came to value especially in the slough of grief.

Still another part of the down-to-earth quality of God's comfort was my discovery during those days after Peter's death that Scripture bathes the subject of death and immortality in the sunlight of normalcy, lifts it out of the realm of the dark and sinister unknown.

One of the reasons Jesus deliberately left the realm of glory to take on the limitations of human flesh for 33 years was so that

> . . . He might deliver and completely set free all those who through the (haunting) fear of death were held in bondage throughout the whole course of their lives.[8]

Part of the process of setting us free is reassurance piled upon reassurance in Scripture that at the death of the physical body, the real person inside lives on without interruption. The Bible tells us that the next life is not only a fully conscious one with every intellectual and spiritual faculty intact but that these faculties are heightened...

> For now we see through a glass, darkly; but then face to face: now I know in part; but then shall I know even as also I am known.[9]

This is the assurance that our loved one will be able to remember, to think, to will, to love, to worship, and to understand so much more on the other side of the barrier of death. Thus our new life will be no sleeping unconscious or unfeeling existence.

In Christ's parable of the rich man and Lazarus, He pictures both men as having a fully conscious life after death, of recollecting earthly life with no break in memory.

Then there are Christ's words from the cross:

> And he (one of the thieves who was being crucified) said unto Jesus, 'Lord, remember me when thou comest into thy kingdom.'
> And Jesus said unto him 'Verily, I say unto thee, Today shalt thou be with me in paradise.'[10]

Christ's promise to the dying thief would have been nonsense had He not meant that after death on that very day, both He and the thief would know themselves to be themselves, would remember that they had suffered together, would recognize each other.

That memorable night at Seaview when the risen Lord had come to me, I had learned first-hand about our spiritual bodies. Now I found the verification in Scripture.

"There is a natural body, and there is a spiritual body," the Apostle Paul tells us. Then he goes on to more detail. This spiritual body will give us much the same recognizable appearance that we have had on earth, except that if imperfect, deformed or diseased, all will be made perfect:

> It (the body) is sown in corruption; it is raised in incorruption: It is sown in dishonor; it is raised in glory: it is sown in weakness; it is raised in power....[11]

Once again, the illness experience had been such perfect preparation for the Valley of the Shadow. How gracious God was to have granted me that fleeting experience of first-hand, practical knowledge about the spiritual body. I knew now how real it is, how vivid are the physical faculties of sight, hearing, speech, thinking, smell, touch—only somehow transferred to the spiritual realm about which we know so little. More, how beautiful will be the casting off of the limitations of flesh and of earth's hampering framework of time and space.

Most of the sorrowing find it necessary to deal with the "what if" stage. I was no exception. Almost always this period of sharp questioning and self-reproach with some guilt mixed in, comes after the first numbness has worn off.

I remember that it was my mother who helped me through this as she sat in the little needlepoint rocker near me and with rare wisdom, simply listened. She offered no advise or pat words of sympathy. It was enough that she was there mourning with me, mixing her tears with mine. Unflinchingly, she allowed me to pour over her the broadside of negative, sometimes bitter thoughts.

After Peter's first so-sudden heart attack in late March l946, had I done everything possible to save my husband? Had it really been God's will that Peter die? Or was this just another failure on my part?

Then I remembered that I had been annoyed with my husband and childishly petulant on the last Sunday of his life. On the way home from church, we had turned on the radio. Just as Peter had brought the car to a halt before our front door, the announcer had mentioned the approaching Saint Valentine's Day.

Peter had reached across for my hand. "Will you be my valentine, Catherine?" he had asked gaily.

And I had withdrawn my hand and ruthlessly crushed his small moment of gaiety by replying sarcastically, "Oh, sure! I'll be your valentine, having a gay time all by myself here in Washington while you're making a speech in Des Moines. I hear you decided to accept that invitation, too."

For a passing moment a look of pain had crossed his face. The remembrance of that look hurt me now.

Between sobs I told Mother of that episode and verbally whipped myself. "How could I have been like that? What on earth got into me? I'm supposed to be a woman—not a child. How could I have been so immature, so disgustingly petty?"

Grief fanned into flame my resentment against all those who had known of Peter's heart condition and yet had persisted in heaping demands on him. These demands had proliferated from 1947 on, after he had become Chaplain of the United States Senate.

"How often I've stood by," I said to Mother, "and heard someone say to Peter in one moment, 'Dr. Marshall, please don't overdo. You just must take care of yourself.' And then in the very next moment, plead with him to speak to their pet group. *Their* organization was always different; their group should always be the exception. How selfish can human beings be?"

Then, having struck out at people, I lashed out again at God. "Why? Why did it have to end this way?" I asked bitterly. "Were Peter and I duped? Has everything that Peter preached been just pious nonsense? If God is a God of love and has the power to help us, why didn't He do something about Peter's heart?"

Sorely troubled, Mother knew any words she might speak would make little difference at the moment. Every bitter thought—against myself and other people and God—had to come up and out.

She understood my need for an answer to the agonizing question every sorrowing person asks, "Where is the God of love who cares about the individual in what has happened?" She also recognized that if I was not allowed to ask this question, get it all out, there could be no healing of my bruised heart; that without this emptying of the bitterness and negativity, I would not later be able to receive the balm of Christ's healing oil. I would either flee life or live it on a busy-busy level, dragging an anesthetized spirit after me.

"In God's own time," she told me quietly, "you will get God's answers."

Mother knew so well that God alone can finally heal the brokenhearted. Grief is a mutilation, a gaping hole in the human spirit. After all, the ties that bind parents to children, brothers to sisters, and husbands to wives are the deepest of bonds, as real as love is real. Some beloved person has been wrested, torn bodily from one's life. The hurt is nonetheless factual even though the family physician cannot clinically prove it; Christ is still the greatest Physician to the spirit.

It was Rebecca Beard, a human doctor, who helped to put my sore heart into the hands of the Great Physician. Several years before, Rebecca had given up her medical practice to work full time in spiritual therapy. When I heard that she was passing through Washington briefly, I sought an appointment with her.

Soon I was pouring out my heart to her—all the hurt of it, the ineptness and the fear I felt about facing the future alone.

At first, as my mother had, this physician-friend just let me talk, saying little, offering no advice for the future. She was a motherly type of woman; sometimes there were tears in her warm eyes as she watched me.

Then finally, when the well of my emotion was dry, she said quietly, "As a doctor, I have only one remedy to offer for what ails you. Let's talk to Jesus about it."

Her prayer was a simple, heartfelt claiming of Christ's promise to bind up the brokenhearted. My heart had been broken and emptied. Now was the time to ask that He take it, make it whole again and fill it up with His love. When the two of us had finished talking to Him, she gathered me in her ample arms. That afternoon His gentle hand was laid on my heart.

And I knew that from that moment the healing had begun somewhere in the depths of my being.

Catherine at Samuel D. Engel's desk, Hollywood (1953)

VII

His
Call To Me

For we are fellow workers for God....
Each man's work will
become manifest; for the day will
disclose it, because it will
be revealed with fire, and the fire
will test what sort of work
each one has done.

I Corinthians 3:9,13—RSV

His Call To Me

The three men from the church were kind, eager to be helpful, but determined that I be realistic about my bleak financial situation. One of them, a knowledgeable insurance agent, had everything neatly worked out on a graph.

"I recommend that you spread Dr. Marshall's insurance over a reasonably long period of time. After all, it will be eight years before Peter John goes to college."

"How much income will we have each month?" I asked.

"One hundred and seventy-one dollars a month for the first eight years. Then the monthly income will take a drop."

"You must be clear-eyed about this, Catherine," chimed in the other businessman. "That won't be enough to maintain your car. You should probably sell it."

"And you're scarcely strong enough yet to hold down a real job," the other friend added. "It's only been two years since you regained health. By the way, what *could* you do job-wise?"

I began to have a suffocating feeling. "I—I don't quite know. I married right out of college—have only a bachelor of arts degree—not even teacher training. I couldn't be a secretary, I don't know shorthand."

The three men had all been Peter's close friends and were genuinely fond of me. Yet they considered me a poor prospect indeed for a bread-earning widow. I could see it in their eyes, feel it in the way they were approaching the subject of finances.

"I don't think you realize how desperate your situation is," one friend insisted, trying to drive home his point. "One hundred and seventy-one dollars a month in Washington won't even cover the bare necessities."

"The Cape Cod cottage is a tangible asset," another added. "I think you should sell it quickly."

The three men left that night distressed because I did not seem fearful enough. They suspected that they had failed to convince me that I was facing a severe financial crisis. They were right. It was not so much a stubborn refusal to accept their gloomy forecasts—financial or otherwise. Rather that even as a protective shield had been thrown over my emotions at the time of Peter's death and for a few days afterward, now I felt that same shield covering my faith regarding the future. It was not my doing; Someone else was sheltering me. Their fear-darts, however well meaning, had simply hit the protective covering and bounced off.

Yet I had not argued with these solicitous friends because facts and figures had substantiated all they had said. There the facts were (as the workaday world sees facts), all down on paper in neat columns and graphs. How could figures lie? Yet somehow I felt that they did lie. Something was missing.

Alone in my room I stared out the window into the moonlight shining on swaying treetops. In so many areas I was naïve, unknowledgeable. At thirty-five I had never in my life figured out an income tax blank, had a car inspected, consulted a lawyer or tried to read an insurance policy. Railroad timetables were an enigma to me. It was a rare occasion indeed when my household checking account balanced. I had never invested any money or braved a trip to the city of New York by myself.

The moonlight outside was almost white. One brilliant star above the treetops winked like a solitaire. Suddenly, standing there at the window, I knew what the missing factor was. My three friends who had meant to be so kind, who saw my many inadequacies, had reckoned without God.

I remembered how often Peter had faced this same attitude with his church officers. He would come home from a trustees' meeting looking sad and grim. "Cath'rine, no matter what's presented for their approval, their litany is always the same, 'But Dr. Marshall, where is the money coming from?' Where's their faith in God?"

But either God was there—I Am That I Am—a fact more real than any figures or any graphs, or He was not. If He was there, then reckoning without Him was certainly not being "realistic"; in fact, it could actually be the most hazardous miscalculation of all.

God had met me in Peter's hospital room that morning only an hour or so after his death. I had felt His Presence, known He was there. And the words He had spoken so clearly to me even as I had been about to leave the room were emblazoned on my consciousness: *Goodness and mercy shall follow you all the days of your life.*

It was His personal pledge to me. In the days ahead and indeed, during all the years to follow, I would hug that promise close to me.

So now I was facing one of those crises—a crossroad of life. I had to walk on into that new life, but which road should I take?

One decision I could make immediately: I would refuse to be destitute. The thrust of Mother's teaching in this

regard had gone deep, so deep. Why should any child of
the King consent to poverty?

So I claimed for Peter John and for me that great promise
that stirs the imagination and sends creativity whirring
into action...

> And we know that all things work together for good
> to them that love God, to them who are the called
> according to His purpose.[1]

How often Peter, in quoting this promise, from the pulpit, had pointed out that God never meant for this "good"
to be limited to spiritual blessing; that He knows perfectly
well our need for rent money and clothes and food.

But now the Spirit was singling out of this promise, His
rhēma for me at this moment—*to them who are the called
according to His purpose.*

I felt a tingling at the top of my spine. Dared I entertain
a hope that He could actually be calling me for a purpose
of His own; was there some special work for *me* to do?

A sense of adventure crept in. It would be exciting to
see what God wanted me to do with my new life. I sensed
that when His grand design for me was revealed in its
entirety, it would include so much more than provision
for economic needs.

But I could never have imagined that His answer to the
"why" of this new life would embody more than just
seeing that Peter's ministry did not die with his mortal
body; that He might want to extend that ministry above
all that I could ask or think or dream, all the while giving
me unimaginable joy in being a part of that.

But meanwhile there were other things I was learning
which I would share in the years ahead with those who
had lost a loved one through death, divorce, or separation.
For one thing, no major decisions should be made in the
weeks immediately following the crisis period. Almost always one experiences deep shock in such separation. Suf-

ficient time must be allowed for recovery before it is possible to have a firm basis for making any decisions.

I was fortunate in not having to make an immediate
selection of where my son and I were going to live. We
were able to stay in the manse for almost ten months while
the church searched for a new pastor. During those
months familiar, beloved, and once-shared possessions
helped to soothe my sore spirit, such as Peter's wildly
turbulent seascapes on the walls of our home and the well-
worn games in the game closet. Being able to walk our
cocker spaniel Jeff, along the same familiar few blocks,
was balm to my spirit rather than added hurt.

Next, I found that the mechanics connected with separation are actually helpful, though they may seem hard.
In the very beginning one may feel that these practical
activities are an intrusion into grief or despair. The
wounded person looks out on the world with new eyes,
marveling that other people on the streets and in the shops
are going on about their business as if nothing has happened, as if everything were just the same.

How is it possible, one wonders at such a time, to force
oneself to sort out dresser and desk drawers; to change
living habits; to rearrange finances; to put one's mind to
business and insurance details; to cope with the dozens
of telephone calls and personal messages, and deal with
the loving concern of friends and family?

The truth is that the empty heart needs work for the
hands to do. I learned that there is a certain therapy in
these necessary mechanics. Peter's church office had to be
emptied of all his possessions. On the self-appointed day
I climbed the stairs to the office and sat down at Peter's
desk. Impulsively I opened the front middle drawer. There
was Peter's date book open to the week of January 23. It
was to have been a busy week. I sat there staring at it.
How precipitously death invades life.

And inserted in the front of the date book was a newspaper clipping with the caption, "Would You Live a Longer Life If You Could?"

I glanced up, and there on the top of one of the bookcases was a carefully detailed model of John Knox's house in Edinburgh. Once Peter and I had walked hand in hand up those narrow steps into that queer little medieval house. "On, memories that bless and burn. . ."

There followed hours of taking Peter's books off the shelves, packing them into boxes. Pictures—a group of etchings, all seascapes, and a fine lithograph of the American flag—had to be taken down and packed, all drawers emptied. Yet as I worked that day there was a strange, sweet easing of my pain.

An entry in my Journal at this time charted my course of action:

> I must use part of my Quiet Time to hear what the Lord has for me to do. He has indicated that He does have a plan for my life. Could it be that my dream of being a writer is part of this plan? I must be open to everything that could lead to this: letters, invitations, counsel of friends.

Several days later a friend wrote to me: ".... the following matter is on my heart and a like sentiment has come my way from various people in the congregation. I, along with thousands, earnestly hope that you will see to it that Peter's sermons, his prayers in the Senate and from his pulpit, will be published."

Soon these requests for a book making some of Peter's sermons and prayers available to everyone were coming at me from all sides.

But I had no contacts in the publishing field. No doubt friends could have been my go-betweens, but I shrank from pushing for this. Therefore, my response was the prayer for a sure sign. "Lord, if this is *Your* plan, then *You* open the door for it. That way I'll *know*."

Within six weeks of this prayer I received letters from three publishers asking the same question: Would I be interested in compiling and editing a book of Peter Marshall's sermons and prayers? It seemed that God's word was "go."

After checking out the publishing houses and conferring with several knowledgeable friends, of the three I chose the Fleming H. Revell Company in New York. A contract was worked out whereby I would edit a minimum of 12 of my husband's sermons for a book to be published in late fall, 1949. A small advance was provided which helped me with living expenses during the next six months.

Peter had left some 600 complete sermon manuscripts filed in three worn, black-and-white cardboard boxes. The proposed book could include at the most only 15 to 20. The problem was, on what basis should I go about trying to choose from the 600?

While the editors at Fleming Revell had caught a whiff of excitement about Peter's preaching, I know now that more deliberate reflection on their part, plus reactions from tough-minded salesmen, had quickly tempered their enthusiasm once I began work on the book. "Fond widow editing preacher's sermons for publication" did not exactly make them envision a best-seller.

A casual or hurried job on my part could have defeated the project or produced a volume with a modest sale at best. But as the editing job progressed, I began to experience the deep satisfaction and inner contentment known only to those who have found the right vocational spot for them.

It was not that my adjustment to bereavement was complete. In fact, it had scarcely begun. But in spite of the empty void inside me, it was as if I had finally come home to my natural habitat.

The work of editing; the virility of the sermon material itself; Peter's extraordinary handling of the English language—his intuitive use of the precise word; his humor;

the instinctive knowledge that people near and far would find these messages food for their hungry spirits; the flashing facets of Peter's personality that leapt from the typewritten pages; the feel of paper and pencil in my hands— every bit of it was pure joy. And gradually I began to see that many things done in the years gone by had been meant as preparation for this task.

During the long quiet days of work on the editing of the manuscripts while Peter John was in school, a scene out of the past came unbidden to my mind, that scene in that room I had loved so—father's study—with books lining the walls floor to ceiling on several sides of the room. In that setting a love for books—for reading them, handling them, collecting them, even the dream of someday writing them, had become a part of my life.

From girlhood, I had been haunted by the dream of writing. In college the desire to write was ever with me. Preparing term papers in English or history was not work, but joy.

Marriage to Peter had postponed the fulfillment of the dream but not erased it. The Christmas after our first trip to Scotland, I had presented Peter with a neatly typed *Journal of a Trip to Scotland*, bound in a handsome leather notebook. The writing had been a labor of love, meant for his eyes alone. Something in me decreed that I had to keep on writing. Whether or not any of it was ever published seemed almost incidental.

Then during the period of illness, a portion of my soul-searching to evaluate the meaning of human life and mine in particular, had been the need to find out whether my girlhood desire to be a writer had been truly a God-given dream:

> If I thought I wanted to be a writer, but what I really wanted was fame or money, or even that my name would not die after me, then this would be false desire. But such I do not believe to be the case.

I have always loved ideas. I've enjoyed trying to express them in as accurate and beautiful a way as possible since I was a little girl. It gives me real soul-satisfaction. . .

After pondering all this for many days, necessarily long quiet days, I had decided that this dream passed the most honest tests I could devise. And just about that time two verses in the New Testament had seemed written in fire:

And this is the confidence that we have in Him, that, if we ask anything according to His will, He heareth us:

And if we know that He hear us, whatsoever we ask, we know that we have the petitions that we desired of Him.[2]

If the wish to be a writer was God's will for me, He would hear me when I asked for the help with it I needed; and if He heard, then this wish would someday be granted. The timing would be up to Him. So I sent this particular dream wafting back toward heaven with the confident awareness that He had already heard.

Now five years later strange events had placed the pencil back in my hands. Deep within me the message came, "There is a fullness of time for all things. This is the fullness of time appointed for your girlhood dream of being an author. This editing and writing is now My call on your new life."

If this work assigned me was truly God's "call," then He would send me to the right persons at the right time to give a special quality to this book of sermons.

At that juncture I remembered something else, another of Peter Marshall's favorite promises, prized because it had been tested and tested again in the crucible of his experience, and never found wanting. . .

"But seek ye first the kingdom of God, and his righteousness; and *all these things* shall be added unto you" (italics added).[3]

For me this had to mean that if I obeyed God's call for a vocation, then "all these things," meaning provision, would follow, simply be "added unto us."

During the next five months I watched unfolding before my wondering eyes that very juxtaposition of ideas, persons, and events for which I had asked God. Then this meticulous intermeshing of so many factors must be what the Apostle Paul had meant by the "working together" for good in that great Romans' promise.

First, a group of young adults in our church wanted to help with the massive job of reading and screening Peter's 600 sermon manuscripts. Sitting around our dining room table, the entire room awash in papers, these were stimulating, sometimes hilarious work sessions.

Someone would break the silence with "You've just *got* to hear this. . .

> 'Church members in too many cases are like deep sea divers, encased in the suite designed for many fathoms deep, marching bravely to pull out plugs in bath-tubs."[4]

A few moments later someone else would begin chuckling...

> Modern politics appear to be related to the art of conjuring. . . The skeletons in the nation's cupboards are replaced by the rabbits that come out of the politicians' hats.[5]

How did Peter ever think of such metaphors and similes?

> It is the same old brass of willful disobedience coated with the chromium of the 20th century.[6]

And then one evening Tom Wharton, a member of the group, made a significant discovery. The text of the sermon pamphlets, which the church had for years been distributing and selling for 10 cents, had been printed in the usual prose style.

But when Tom compared a passage from one of these pamphlets with the comparable passage in the typed manuscript Peter had carried into the pulpit with him, Tom was startled at the difference. The words of the typed copy sprang alive on the page. One could all but hear the sound of Peter's voice. The reader caught the same emphasis of word and clause that the oral delivery had supplied. And the extra amount of white space (for in the typed sermons the copy looked rather like blank verse) made reading sermons a delight rather than a chore.

There followed days of testing this out by typing a number of passages both ways and then trying them out on a variety of people.

The pamphlet form looked like this:

> To know great art—the red of Titian, the sunsets of Turner, the seas of Winslow Homer; to have felt the spell of epic heroisms; to have swung to the rhythmic pulse of Homer; to have known the tenderness of Francis of Assisi; to engrave the prologue to the Gospel of John on the heart; and to march with the majestic affirmations of the Nicene Creed: It does something inside a man. It stretches him mentally, stirs him morally, inspires him spiritually....[7]

But the typed sermon looked so different, so alive:

To know great art—the reds of Titian. . .
     the sunsets of Turner. . .
     the seas of Winslow Homer. . .
To have felt the spell of epic heroisms. . .
     to have swung to the rhythmic pulse of Homer. . .
     to have known the tenderness of St. Francis of Assisi. . .

To engrave the prologue to the Gospel of John on the heart... to march with the majestic affirmations of the Nicene Creed:

It does something inside a man.
It stretches him mentally. . .
    stirs him morally. . .
        inspires him spiritually. . .

All our readers agreed: the stair-step device which Peter used only for his own delivery would make all the difference on the printed page. The unanimous decision was that the Creator-God was at this point leading us to something new in publishing.

But then I faced the question, how could I present such an innovative (and probably expensive) typesetting idea to an old, conservative publishing house? Still, if an Omnipotent God was guiding this, He would see to its acceptance.

He did. The Revell Company agreed to try it. I learned later that they almost immediately regretted their decision since the stair-step arrangement of the words demanded a great deal of thought about book design, compounded the copyreader's task of marking the manuscript for the printer, typesetting problems and so forth.

Meanwhile our efforts and prayers were stirring interest in the book throughout the country the way ripples spread out in a pond after a stone is dropped into the water. Attention to small details pays dividends. When each person involved in a project communicates to others, a chain-reaction effect results.

Catching wind of this, I was dismayed to find that a first printing of only 10,000 copies had been ordered for the book to be published under the title of *Mr. Jones, Meet the Master*. I protested to the head of the Revell Company that they should print at least 25,000.

Mr. Barbour, then elderly, had been a publisher for a long time. He was not a tall man. But as he drew himself up to his full height, he seemed to tower over me. "*Mrs.* Marshall," his voice was scathing, "*everyone* in publishing knows that posthumus sermons never sell."

With that, he closed the subject.

One final decision remained. An Introduction to *Mr. Jones* was needed. Whom should we ask? The publisher felt that some national figure and a prominent friend of Peter's, like Senator Kenneth Wherry or Senator Arthur Vandenberg, should be invited to write it. I refused to believe that Peter's material needed a "name" to launch it.

Moreover, it seemed to me that an altogether different sort of Introduction was needed for Peter Marshall's sermons. The readers should have a thumbnail sketch of Peter's flavorsome personality, including his refusal to be stereotyped in Washington where political and power stereotype has long been the order of the day. And the sketch should include Peter's strong tastes and convictions, even his goofs and idiosyncracies. I felt that I alone could write a prologue like that.

Next question: How to present *that* idea to the by-this-time somewhat weary executives of the Revell Company? I sensed that these publishers looked on me as a sentimental widow without either writing talent or experience, bitten with grandiose ideas about "her" book as she sought to idealize her dead husband.

So I approached them cautiously, "Would you be willing," I asked over the phone, "to let me put on paper the Introduction I have in mind? If you don't like it, then you can throw it in the wastebasket and go ahead with other plans."

There was an almost audible gasp of relief at the other end of the line. On these no-lose terms, Revell agreed to my attempting to set something on paper.

One night, sitting propped up in bed, with the floor awash in papers, I wrote a seven-page sketch of Peter Marshall, the man. I called it "Here Is Peter Marshall" and sent it off to New York.

Two days later the publisher telephoned me. There was undisguised surprise in his voice. "Three of us have read

your Introduction. We didn't think you—that is, well, I
mean, it couldn't be more perfect. Of course we want to
use it."

Those seven pages of original writing turned out to be
my foot in the door of the publishing world.

The first printing of 10,000 copies of *Mr. Jones, Meet the
Master* was sold out before Publication Day was over. For
the next year the publisher enlisted help from several print-
ers to meet the demands for the book. There was no point
in any "I told you so." Rather, I knew that it was cause
for rejoicing.

When informed that *Mr. Jones* was to make *The New York
Times* best-seller list, I was not as impressed as I should
have been. For me, the real success of the book was measured in an altogether different way—by the hundreds of
letters that were pouring in trying to express to me what
the messages of the sermons were meaning in the lives of
men and women.

The success of *Mr. Jones, Meet the Master* led to Edward
Aswell, then editor-in-chief at the McGraw-Hill Book Company, reaching out for me. He had in mind a second book
of sermons. Instead, I suggested that the story of the man
behind the sermons needed to be told.

Mr. Aswell responded favorably to that idea but following an editor's usual procedure, asked to see an outline
of the book I had in mind, together with a chapter or two
and/or sample segments of manuscript.

By then Peter John and I had settled into "Waverley",
the Cape Cod cottage for the summer. For days I struggled
with an outline, a chore in which I am not adept.

One evening after I had gone to bed, a thought pierced
my mind like a stroke of lightning—the real significance
of the last words Peter had spoken to me on this earth.

The scene vividly before me, I turned on the bedside light, grabbed a pencil and pad off the nightstand and began to write feverishly to transfer it to paper... The setting, the front hall in our Cathedral Avenue home in Washington; the time three a.m., January 25. Parked on the street outside, the ambulance waited to take Peter to the hospital. I longed to go with him, but could not since that would have left Peter John alone in the big house.

Peter had looked up at me from the stretcher which the orderlies had set down for a moment. He must have known more surely than I the import of this moment. All the love in his eyes reached out for me. "Cath'rine," the words were gentle, yet somehow triumphant, "see you, darling, see you in the morning."

Why had I never thought of this before? "See you in the *morning*. No, not just any dawning, no ordinary day. Within the strange providence of a loving Father (whose plan I still could not understand, only accept), I would see Peter again on that other bright Morning, beyond pain, beyond time.

I wrote it, only a page and a half, with tears streaming down my face, splashing onto the page.

The following day, with relief, I shifted mood altogether and wrote part of a humorous chapter about Peter's foibles and eccentricities, and some occasions when he had botched it up with some of the overly-conservative church ladies quite unable to understand the unsanctimonious exuberance of their young Scottish minister.

The two pieces of manuscript along with my defective outline were then mailed off to Edward Aswell.

The day came when I stood in the tiny West Harwich village postoffice and found a letter from Mr. Aswell. Eagerly, I tore it open. Two sentences in the second paragraph leapt off the typed page...

"We shall be proud to publish this book. I am going to send you a contract immediately."

That book was *A Man Called Peter*.

With the writing of this book God fulfilled my dream of becoming a full-fledged author. And once again, He blessed the book with sales beyond my wildest imagination. *A Man Called Peter* stayed on *The New York Times* bestseller list for more than 50 consecutive weeks, something of a record.

Over the years fifteen books have followed. Often I pause to marvel at the way He has led me: my joyous fulfillment in the writing itself; the fact that what is shared on paper is of help and inspiration to others, and the dividend of this work assigned me by God taking care of all economic needs. Who but God could even plan such an amalgam!

We did not sell the car until it was time to trade it in for another one. We kept *Waverley,* the Cape Cod cottage, and Peter John and I and our friends enjoyed it summer after summer.

After not quite two years in a cramped apartment in McLean Gardens, a large apartment complex in northwest Washington, we bought a modest home just off Wisconsin Avenue between Georgetown and Bethesda. We suffered no economic deprivation, never had to borrow money. Not a single one of the kind businessmen's gloomy forecasts ever came true. The monthly insurance checks were nice to have, a loving, reassuring gift from Peter to his family, but we never had to live on insurance income alone.

Reckon without God? To do so would be as nonsensical as ignoring the sun as we watch a shifting pattern of sunlight and shadow on the ground.

Reckon without God? We'd better not, not in any area of life, if we are serious about knowing reality and about achieving our full potential. For our God never considers our work as merely a way to earn a living—so much an hour, so much a year. He has given each of us the gift of life with a specific purpose in view. To Him work is a sacrament, even what we consider unimportant, mundane work. When done "as unto the Lord," it can have eternal significance.

It is therefore important to Him that we discover what our particular aptitudes and talents are; then that we use those talents to His glory and their maximum potential during our all-too-brief time on earth.

For each of us, He does have a plan. What joy to find it and even out of our helplessness, let Him guide us in its fulfillment.

Catherine and Peter John on the beach, Cape Cod

VIII

Single Parent

For the Lord your God....
executes justice for the
fatherless and widows....
Fear not, for you shall not
be ashamed; neither be confounded
and depressed....For your Maker
is your husband, the Lord of hosts
is His name....

Deuteronomy 10:17,18;
Isaiah 54:4,5—Amplified

Single Parent

Peter John had just turned nine when his father died. I can still see his stricken face when he heard the news and feel his trembling body as I knelt down to take him in my arms. There were just the two of us now—mother and son.

Still, after the first state of shock, young Peter seemed to be bearing the loss of a father so much better than I was taking the loss of a husband. He asked such boyish questions as, "Who will help me finish my train set?" "Where will we live now?" "Will I have to change schools?" "Can I still join the Boy Scouts?"

The questions seemed so normal that at the time I did not realize the noxious brew of anxiety, loneliness, desolation, even anger the questions were covering up. Few children can articulate the real issue underneath the anger, "If God loves me, then why did He take away my daddy?" With a very young child, there can also be an irrational juvenile reaction that would never occur to an adult: "If my daddy (mother) really loved me, then why would he (she) die and leave me?" In either instance this anger is stuffed down into the unconscious to emerge as rebellion and hostility toward authority at some future time.

In the years since, I have learned that in divorce situations there is often hidden anger against the parent who the child feels is most responsible for the break-up. Also, sometimes guilt in the child... *"Did I do something wrong to help to drive Mommy (or Daddy) away?"*

I sensed none of this happening to my son. Carefully, he was included in the planning arrangements and in every part of his father's funeral. Repeated attempts were made to explain death and immortality to Peter John. He seemed to understand. Here again, adults often assume a comprehension simply not there.

Too shy and fearful to bare the heart (I too had been like that in childhood), my son became quiet and indrawn. Pictures of him during this period show a sad, strained face. Obviously, I was not sufficiently aware of his inner desolation during these months of adjustments and thus failed him at this point.

How should a single parent handle such a situation? I know now that we should never give up easily in our efforts at dialogue with the child. At meals I would ask questions about Peter's activities at school or play and get one-word answers: "Fine." "Okay." "Good." Of course these were phony answers, an effort to head off deeper probing into painful areas.

As time went on during our limping dinner-table efforts at conversation, I would get the mental picture of a boy crouching behind a stone wall, peering over now and again, but afraid to come out.

Afraid of what? That he would be hurt further in honest confrontation? Afraid to stop crouching behind the wall and join the human race?

I sought the advice of counselor after counselor, had session after session, but we could neither find the way to bring down that wall, or to make Peter come out from what he regarded as his only protection.

At other times as when the two of us would be driving the five hundred plus miles to Cape Cod, always I struggled to find subjects of interest to my son. After receiving monosyllabic responses, I would give up and retreat into my own thought world, somewhat to the relief of Peter, I sensed.

Many times my son would then find a ball game on the car radio. To me these were interminably boring affairs. "Ball one, strike one. . ." "Ball two, strike two. . ." "Ball three. . ." "Ball four." Every now and then there would be a flurry of action, but the droning of balls and strikes and other unrelated information seemed to be nine-tenths of the verbage. *Who cares,* I would ask myself, *whether the pitcher first scratched his left ear, then his right thigh, then shifted his feet three times while he was winding up?* How could such repetitious commentary possibly interest a young boy?

In an effort to relate, I forced myself to go to baseball, football, and hockey games with my son. Baseball to me was always excruciatingly slow and boring, with the players constantly chasing after, throwing, or swinging a bat at a small, white ball. How was it that thousands upon thousands of people could get so worked up about it?

Football seemed to be in the category of bloody bull-fights. Men throwing themselves ferociously at one another, sometimes even knocking each other unconscious. The idea that countless millions of people could go into a frenzy of shrieking excitment about the progress of a melon-sized, brown ball moving up and down the field was more than I could comprehend. My only consoling thought was, *"If this can serve the male as a substitute for war, then it would be worth all the national time and energy and millions of dollars expended".*

Ice hockey was more enjoyable. At least the speed and grace of the skaters was exhilerating to watch. But again the vicious body contact made me wince. My mistake was in not trying harder to get interested in these sports so that Peter and I could talk about them together. The key to this for me, I later discovered, was the human-interest side of sports, learning the names of the players, how good they were, how much money they made, something of their family life.

There were other ways open to me in helping my son grow up without a father. One was to bring him into contact with other men as much as I could. My dad spent many hours with young Peter, trying to teach him to handle tools and do odd jobs around the house. My brother Bob could talk Peter's sports language and the two of them worked on many a handicraft project together. One Christmas they made most of their gifts. I received a bird house replete with a television antenna and rambling roses painted over the birds' front door hole. The pièce de résistance went to the Hoskins girls, Peter's cousins—a marvelous toy chest decorated inside and out with fairy-tale castles and characters copied from Peter's books.

All of this was to the good, but there was never enough of it. It takes a great deal of masculine companionship to make up for missing a father's steady presence in the everydayness of life.

My experience in this regard would indicate that our church fellowships fail to pick up a God-ordained responsibility in relation to widows. The many references to widows in Scripture indicate that this ministry—spiritual, financial, and help in child rearing—is important to God. Apparently the early New Testament church took seriously this ministry to widows and to their children. For instance:

> Now in these days when the disciples were increasing in number, the Hellenists, murmured against the Hebrews because their widows were neglected in the daily distribution.[1]

> Religion that is pure and undefiled before God and the Father is this: to visit orphans and widows in their

affliction, and to keep oneself unstained from the world.[2]

How much it would mean to these bereft children today, each to become a part of some father's "bundle," as the Quakers say, as a sort of surrogate father!

The need is more and more urgent. Present estimates are that in the United States, forty-five percent of all children born in any given year will live with only one of their parents at some time before they are eighteen. In 1980 children of divorce (minors) numbered eleven million, with at least a million more added every year. One can scarcely imagine the discouragement and neediness of all these single parents, not to mention the confusion and bitterness of the children involved.

In my situation the best answers to the sense of helplessness and frustration came through my early morning Quiet Time when in prayer I would seek God's guidance for my son. One entry in my Journal read:

> I am to make a date with Peter John to go over finances. Through this he will begin to feel needed.
>
> I am to begin to praise him more. Try the power of praise for him a lot more often.
>
> Question: What is he to do on Friday and Saturday nights? There has to be real planning ahead on this.

On another occasion when I was feeling very low, I wrote down this guidance I felt God was giving me:

> Do not be afraid for young Peter. No harm will come to him. He also is My child. *I* love him more than you do!

But it was hard to overcome my fears for Peter John as he moved into the teen years. When I caught him smoking cigarettes at age fourteen, I was devastated. My anger erupted and he retreated into sullen silence. When I stormed heaven about my inadequacies as a mother, I wrote down this answer:

> You have still not completely released Peter to Me. Don't strain too much after it though. It will come gradually, if you let Me do it—even as a plant grows under My care, so a child grows.

That summer I was upset because Peter wanted to spend most of the summer visiting friends. An invitation to be with a friend at a seaside resort brought the issue to a head.

One morning in my Quiet Time, I had this answer:

> The business of why Peter doesn't want to go to camp is directly related to the fact that you do not want him to go visiting a friend for five days away from you. You fear the unknown quantity here, the part you can't control and keep your fingers on. In the same way Peter fears the unknown situations he would have to face in camp.

> My answer to you is that these five days when Peter is at the seaside resort will be good practice for you in really trusting Me. When I promise you specifically that I will take over a situation, *I take it over.* Moreover, I can be with Peter every minute, whereas you cannot.

> Remember that worry and trust just don't mix. When Peter leaves you, he will be in My hands and there must be no more worry.

One day while cleaning Peter's room I found a stack of sex-saturated paperback novels. How was I to deal with this? My first inclination was to let my anger boil over and explode. The inner voice said there was a better way.

Quietly that evening I asked him if there was any real reason why he felt it necessary to seek out this kind of reading. He shrugged. "All the kids at school are reading them," was his reply.

This led into a discussion of peer pressure which he picked up and talked about quite freely. He admitted that being accepted by others was far too important to him, that therefore he was inclined to be a follower of what the crowd did. At the end of our discussion, on his own volition, Peter threw the paperbacks into the trash.

But the problem of peer pressure at school began a new period of fear in me. Not sharp fear, more a spiritual unrest which would come to me upon occasion, vague and undefinable, like a splinter in one's soul. One night I asked God what this feeling was all about and what I should do about it. This is the message I got:

> You are fearful for Peter because of deep-hidden guilt concerning him. Fear usually comes from guilt. You feel instinctively—and rightly so—that where you fail to supply strong enough discipline, then I, Peter's heavenly Father, will have to permit those disciplines to be supplied by hard and difficult circumstances. Not enough parents face up to this.
>
> You must quietly get My mind and direction about Peter in these areas and then *act* upon My guidance. As you do act, your fear will leave. But let Me warn you about this. Don't let your time with Me or what I am telling you lull you into a sense of false security or be a substitute for action—or the fear will return in full force.
>
> Here are My instructions:
>
> 1. TV and movies: You are to keep a careful check on what he sees. Plan ahead. Be so well informed about films and TV programs that you will earn Peter's respect in this regard. Where there is no good movie on a Saturday, some other activity must be planned ahead. Often you have taken the line of least resistance because you haven't been prepared with adequate information.
>
> 2. Tidiness and taking care of his own clothes: Insist that he take responsibility here.

3. Money, allowance, etc.: You have not been handling this properly. You must take time—over and over—to come back to Me to think these matters through.

For a period of months there was a big improvement in Peter's and my relationship. Children thrive under structure, and I was being given daily guidance on how to plan ahead and use consistent discipline.

Then came a major disappointment in connection with my writing and for weeks I was bogged down in discouragement. Schedules slipped; there was a period of spiritual drought.

Finally a breakthrough came with a decision made about my next literary project. Now I could get my house back in order. I remember the sense of inner elation I had looking forward to Monday morning when I could get up at 6:30 a.m. for a quiet hour with the Lord.

At 7:30 that morning the telephone rang. "This is Detective C of the Eighth Precinct, Juvenile Squad," he began gently. "Your son, Peter John Marshall, and three other boys got into trouble last Saturday night. They are being accused of taking school property (two axes and a fire extinguisher) and breaking the headlights of two school buses."

I began trembling as he talked. When he told me that I was to appear with Peter John at the Eighth Precinct station at 3:30 that afternoon, my throat was almost too dry to respond.

No members of my family were nearby, so I called several church friends for prayer support. I asked Peter to stay home from school so that we could talk through what had happened. He was defensive and communicated only the bare details. He and some friends had been messing around the school and a few back alleys nearby. They hadn't meant to destroy any property. "Honest!"

Later as I prayed alone, I saw that I could be in danger of being too pridefully concerned about what the publicity might do to my reputation as a Christian. So many people had put my family and me on a pedestal. Would such publicity hurt Christ's cause?

I wept and then remembered Romans 8:28, *All things work together for good to those who love God, to those who are the called according to His purpose.* I would concentrate on this promise.

Peter and I were at Eighth Precinct station from 3:30 until 6:30. As we waited nervously for the two men from the juvenile board to arrive, I have a vivid remembrance of the scene... the dirt in the corners of the room; the man representing the school, whose name ironically enough was Peter, had large luminous brown eyes, black hair peppered with gray, was wearing tennis shoes on a winter's day, and his clothes didn't match; the sad, shocked face of the father of one of the other boys, his eyes like those of a hurt animal.

One of the boys (the son of the man whose eyes revealed so much) put his head down on the table and cried, very softly, trying not to attract attention. Since a very little boy, I learned later, he had wanted to get into West Point. If this went on his record, he would never get there... There was the lined, seamed face of the mother of another boy, holding the little family dog by one of her son's neckties—a strange leash indeed.

Peter's face was tense. Not in a long time had I heard him snap to and say, "Sir." His blond complexion seemed to have a permanent blush. He kept chewing on his fingernails long after there was no bit of surplus nail to chew. When the decision was finally made to let the boys off lightly because they were first offenders, he was relieved but deeply sober.

I was impressed with the way the District of Columbia handled these first offenders. Each boy, with his parents, had to appear before a judge. As I remember it, these were private sessions. When Peter and I appeared before a kindly judge for our talk, to my surprise the judge raised the issue I had considered too prideful. "Peter, your father stood for something in the greater Washington community. You have a proud heritage. Don't tarnish it. Son, I want you to think deeply about all this."

In the aftermath of this episode, I saw that the wall between young Peter and me was in part my doing. The wall remained because I had failed to share with Peter at the depth of spirit. Our whole relationship had been pitched too much on the level of daily schedules, material things—all the superficialities of life between a mother a her 16 year-old son.

Was it too late to change this? I would try. The inner Voice instructed me to open the deeps of my own life and feelings to Peter and share with him. How much he would understand, I could not know. My business was to *obey*. God would have to take care of the rest.

There were no more crises involving Peter during the rest of that school year. Still, I drove to Richmond, Virginia for a conference with a fine Christian educator. He was a man especially knowledgeable about teenage boys and about the best secondary schools. Having heard me out and prayed with me, his advice was that at age 16, Peter needed male authority figures in his life; that therefore, a Christian boys' school was probably indicated for his senior year in high school.

Back home I continued to pray for God's guidance on this.

During these days a friend told me bluntly, "Sons in their teens are always difficult for their mother. When it's time for them to leave home, that's it. You'll get no more than glimpses of them after that."

In my morning time I heard the same thing in a somewhat different way:

> You have done all you can just now. The time has
> come to relinquish your son. Others will take over the
> role of parents in his life. You must accept this as natural
> and trust Me.

So what God wanted seemed clear. After investigating and visiting several schools recommended by the educator, in the end Peter and I settled on the one at the top of the advisor's list—the Mount Hermon School in northwestern Massachusetts. Peter was happy with the choice.

Even so, my spirit was heavy as we packed the car that September day for the drive to Massachusetts. Peter had obtained his driver's license and insisted that he drive. Now over six feet tall, he so towered over me that I felt almost intimidated by his size.

As we drove there was little conversation between us. As usual, he was listening to a baseball game on the radio.

My mind kept wandering from the battle between the Braves and the Giants—or was it the Indians and the Yankees? Much to Peter John's disgust, I could never keep these intrepid warriors straight.

When that certain moment for a good-by was upon us in our rooms in the inn the next day, I was not big enough to take it alone. But I knew where to go for help. Besides, don't all such moments need a benediction?

I tried to keep my heart from showing—not because I was afraid of the heart, but because I didn't want to embarrass Peter John.

"We should be pushing off for school," I said. "But first, would you indulge me in something? This is a significant day for us both. Would you be willing for us to have a prayer together and ask God's blessing on it?"

Peter nodded a little impatiently, so I made the prayer brief. The moment hung in space—passed. But there was the unmistakable feeling in the prayer that we were not two, but three with "Big Peter" a part in this intercession around the throne of God—united across barriers that were no barriers.

Silently, my son picked up his suitcases.

I was a little disappointed in the room at school—circa 1890, golden oak woodwork, the floors well worn by generations of boys' feet, battered furniture, two small windows almost covered with a summer's growth of ivy.

But Peter did not seem to mind. He had just met his roommate, Bruce, and liked him—as blond as he, also a senior. This room would be their digs—their very own. What did 19th century scuffed oak woodwork and worn floors matter?

When Bruce's parents arrived I noticed how his mother, all unconsciously, leaned on her husband's arm, smiling up into his face. *An intact family*, I thought. *How wonderful it must be.*

Next Bruce's mother opened one of his suitcases and carried new shoes and galoshes to the closet, then piles of underwear and pajamas to his chest of drawers.

"I sat up until two last night sewing on name tags," she told me. "Can you imagine these boys acually getting their own laundry together each week—and on time?"

"No—I can't. I suppose they'll learn."

She eyed the iron beds. "Bruce, can't I make your bed for you one last time? You never get it smooth."

"Never mind, Mom, I'll do it myself—later."

She was acting out what I was feeling... the apron strings almost severed but the hands aching to perform a last chore or two. Yet she had three other sons, and Bruce was not the oldest. She had been through this before.

Peter looked at me. He knew, too—knew beyond his years. He said with hesitant dismissal, as if uneasy to have me there longer, "I think you'd better go now, Mom."

So I shook hands with Bruce and his parents, stood on tiptoe to hug my tall son, and walked out—down the worn, uneven steps.

Another era was over. I had parted with my husband. In a very real sense, I had just parted with my son. This was the beginning of his life on his own.

As I drove away, I was thinking, *So to what do I return now? An empty house? Greater loneliness than ever?*

A sudden rainstorm came up, the car's jerky windshield wipers keeping pace with my jumbled, gloomy thoughts.

Ten minutes later that rain ceased as quickly as it had come. I was driving into the setting sun, and the sun had turned the droplets of rain on the windshield into glittering globules of light.

Then to my astonishment, a rainbow appeared, every gorgeous color of the spectrum in its wide perfect arc.

The rainbow of promise. After the great flood in the days of Noah, the writers of Scripture tell us that God first sent the rainbow as His pledge of an

> "everlasting covenant between God and every living creature of all flesh. . ."[3]

> His promise, His covenant: ". . .for lo, I am with you always. . ."

Then I could forget my fears of returning to an empty house, dump by the roadside all my "what ifs" about this new era. *He would be there.*

The rainbow of Promise shimmered and beckoned.

IX

Loneliness

....trust God....when temptation
comes, He will provide
the way out of it....

....The God who did not spare
His own Son but gave Him up
for us all, surely He will give us
everything besides!....What can
ever part us from Christ's love?

I Corinthians 10:13
Romans 8:32,35—Moffatt

Loneliness

The years immediately after young Peter went away to school, first to Mount Hermon then to Yale, were the most difficult of my widowhood. We had finally sold *Waverley*, the Cape Cod cottage, since it was now obvious that Peter would seldom be there. The idea of living alone however, did not frighten me. I have never resisted this. In fact, I prefer being alone for long stretches of the day, as when I am writing in the mornings. But there is a big difference between aloneness and loneliness.

Loneliness is the aching need inside one to share one's life with another. Yet there are other wholesome relationships for single people outside of marriage where the aching void inside oneself can be satisfied. My question now was, what kind of life did God want for me?

During the first years after Peter's death I was convinced that it would be impossible for me ever to marry again, that this would violate something very precious my husband and I had had together. But as the years passed, I began praying about this matter simply by asking questions, by telling God that I did not even know for what it was right to ask. In this way I could leave entirely up to Him the decision as to whether I should ever remarry.

But that seemed a sloppy way of praying. Surely I needed to know myself better than that, what my own deep desires were. Knowing those, then I could at least present them to Him for approval or disapproval.

My growing loneliness was brought into sharp focus the night of a mother-daughter banquet for which I had agreed to make an informal after-dinner talk. Before my part in the program, a young baritone rose to sing a group of semi-classical songs. The last in the group was "Drink to Me Only with Thine Eyes."

I had heard Ben Jonson's words sung many times. They held no special memories for me, nor had I ever felt in the least sentimental about this song....

> Drink to me only with thine eyes,
>   And I will pledge with mine;
> Or leave a kiss within the cup,
>   And I'll not ask for wine.
> The thirst that from the soul doth rise
>   Doth ask a drink divine....

But toward the end of the song, suddenly I felt myself tighten. I was aware that my hands, hidden under the edge of the tablecloth, were clutching the evening bag in my lap until my fingers ached.

This won't do, I thought. *I'll just have to stop listening and deliberately think about something less sentimental.* My eyes roamed over the scene before me—the mothers in their finery with their daughters sitting beside them at the round tables, all listening intently to the tall young singer. I noticed a red-headed teenager's hairdo. Deliberately I studied it, trying to decide how some beautician had created the sleek turned-under effect.

By the time the last notes of the song had died away, the tension in my hands had relaxed, the fullness in my

throat had disappeared. I was able to get to my feet calmly
and even put some humor into my talk.

But this experience had stirred something within me of
which I had been only hauntingly aware. I saw myself
standing before an altar being married again. And every
shred of me protested. Would that not be a betrayal of the
husband who had had all my heart's love—therefore, a
betrayal of the love itself?

Suddenly I knew that such a thing would never be possible except by an act of God changing my thinking, changing something deep inside that was an integral part of my
being.

Several days later I made this notation:

> I must realize that loneliness, that sense of dissatisfac-
> tion, that feeling of some happiness just eluding me,
> is in all human beings, and is put there by God to keep
> us searching after Him. Perhaps when I just "settle
> down" to this doubtful state of single blessedness, in-
> ner peace will come. We shall see.

Even five or six years after Peter's death I found that my
journey through the valley was still a running battle with
self-pity. Several of the couples on our street would often
take a stroll in the early evening. Sometimes seeing them,
I would think, *Were Peter still with me, he and I would be the
youngest couple on this street. But no, our marriage is over.* Or
at the theatre I would see a gray-haired man reach for his
wife's hand, and I would wince with a passing pang of
self-pity.

Or at a dinner party I would find myself the only single
person there. Always I knew that my hostess had not
meant to be thoughtless. It is hard for anyone who has
known only an unbroken family to imagine how this particular situation makes the single person feel. Try as I
might to overcome it, I would find that being in the presence of couples threw my aloneness into sharpest
perspective.

What then is the solution? It must lie somewhere in the realm of relationship. As solitaries we can wither and die. We long to be needed; we yearn to be included; we thirst to know that we belong to someone. The question is—how can we achieve that sense of belonging?

There is a price to be paid. The first tribute exacted is a modicum of honesty with ourselves. On the one hand, do we want to be rid of loneliness so much that we will allow ourselves no more wallowing in the luxury of pity-parties? On the other hand, how badly do we want to make connection with other people? For let's admit it, there are pluses in having only oneself to think of.

In the light of honest answers to questions like these, I decided I need not be lonely unless I chose to be. The first step was recognizing the necessity for a new dimension and the decision to perform a freshening-up on myself. Having to make many public appearances forced me to review my clothes situation. I found a specialist who, after studying my present wardrobe, my figure and my features, skillfully advised me on clothes shopping, even on the right selection for a variety of situations such as certain platform and television appearances.

Then came some quiet reappraisal of certain restrictions my parents had placed upon me in my growing-up years. They had been so full of love for me that the taboos they had put on activities like ballroom dancing and bridge had mattered little to me—then.

But now as a widow in sophisticated Washington, I was embarrassed when someone asked me to dance. Or I had to decline an invitation to play bridge with friends.

The answer was to learn how—and I did. I enrolled for a series of lessons in ballroom dancing. Then three women friends and I set aside an evening a week to master bridge. We spread out teaching manuals on a second table beside us and learned the game together by playing it.

Seven years after Peter's death a change was taking place inside me without my being aware of it. While resigned to widowhood in my mind, emotionally I was preparing myself for a new kind of life. This entry appears in my Journal at about this time:

> God does want me to be happy. God does want Peter John to be well-adjusted and happy. God has made me the way I am, has made me for happiness and love; I do not believe that He means or wants me to stay by myself for the rest of my life.

Odd, how as soon as I opened the inner door, outer doors began swinging open too. Men began seeking me out for dates—a procession of them. Widowers—one a college president, one an insurance agent, older bachelors, a wealthy California citrus-grower, a Washington professor, a Texas investment broker. Then there was the businessman I met while giving a dinner talk to a university convention at the Mayflower Hotel in Washington. Tall, slim, distinguished-looking, I liked him immediately.

I learned that Howard was a widower with two teenage boys, his wife having died of cancer the previous year. He was from a wealthy, influential southern family and had political aspirations.

Howard invited me out for lunch, then dinner, then for a weekend at his large family estate in South Carolina where his sister was the hostess. I was impressed, and Howard and his two sons seemed to like me.

I confessed in my Journal:

> The revelation today is that there has to be someone else for me into whose life I can pour everything. Since this is what my whole being cries out for, it is as sure of fulfillment as that the tides of the ocean will come in again. Somewhere there is a man whose life needs this lavish giving, whose personality and career will bloom and blossom under it. Whether that man be Howard, only God knows at this point—though my heart says "yes."

If there were pangs inside me that my sudden interest in Howard was a betrayal of Peter's memory, they did not last long....

> Today God gave me a beautiful gift, namely, the assurance that remarriage is *His* idea not mine. *He* wants it for me even more than I want it. But a gift is not truly ours until we take it.

> So I accept it with greatest gratitude. This means that I no longer have to worry about whether it's right to marry again; all I do have to do is to give thanks to God that the matter is settled and relax until God's time comes to meet "the man."

> I see that only now—after almost seven years—am I finally ready really to accept Peter's death fully, really ready to shut the door on the past and go out into a new life. Obviously, remarriage couldn't happen until this step was taken on my part. No man wants to be part of my old life. It's incredible perhaps that it has taken me so long to come to this position.

Howard was appointed to a high position in Washington and moved into an office in the Pentagon. As we saw each other more often, I became aware of some unsettling qualities in him. He tended to avoid any discussions about Christianity. I sensed that any faith he had was a sort of inherited social grace with nothing personal about it. He seemed overly fond of the superficialities of life—eating, drinking, clothes, cars and so on. He was restless and ill at ease whenever other people paid attention to me in regard to my books. Yet his charm, dignity, and statesmanlike approach to issues appealed to me. And he did have a warm, affectionate nature.

Questions about Howard kept arising in my journals:

> My guidance is that I am to leave entirely up to him and God if or when he will read *A Man Called Peter*; that I am to make no hints about this or try to encourage him to read it.

God has big things in store for Howard. In the next
year or two he will lose his frustrations as he loses
himself in something bigger than himself. I have a vision for him; so does God.

Howard began to do a lot more traveling and I saw less
and less of him. He would call and explain the heavy new
responsibilites laid upon him. I made this comment in my
Journal:

The real explanation of Howard's lack of initiative at
the present time is that he is *afraid* of becoming involved
with me. He's not ready for it; he senses that it is dy-
namite. God tells me to be patient under this and to
try to understand it.

Short notes began coming periodically from Howard
with foreign postmarks: Geneva, London, Rome, Bonn.
I was reminded of the long periods of silence I suffered
during my three years of courtship with Peter.

Then one day I ran into Howard unexpectedly in the
corridor of the Pentagon. He was startled; so was I. I stammered out an explanation of why I was there, a trifle too
defensively.

"It's really good to see you, Catherine." He seemed
over-hearty. We talked a few minutes, then he went on
to a meeting.

As he walked away I was annoyed at myself for being
so thrown off balance. I doubted that even a meeting with
the President himself would have rattled me to such an
extent. And of course it had to be poise that Howard ad-
mired so much.

The next entry reflected all this:

I have felt more detached from Howard lately. Is my
feeling for him just a bundle of infatuation? If his influential position were removed, if his wealth and his
relative youth (about 50 I would judge) were all removed, would I then still fancy myself in love with the
man himself?

Then I would get provoked with myself and lack of patience and pour out my feelings and any new insights:

> God is Sovereign in this whole situation. Howard's actions and decision—and mine—are truly in God's hands. I am God's and have given my life into His care and keeping. I am to accept Howard's silences and what has *not* happened in recent weeks as having come directly from God's hands.

> I am to offer God the sacrifice of thanksgiving by thanking Him for all these unwelcome circumstances. This is the proof, the acting out of my faith in His Omnipotence.

That June a letter came from Howard after a silence of several months. It was a short note. He wanted me to hear the news directly from him, rather than any other source, he wrote. He was to be married again. The woman was the daughter of a general, a widow with three small children.

When the letter came I thought I had already relinquished the whole matter. Apparently, not so. There was a surprising emotional backwash. I did no serious writing for weeks.

My secretary Peg came to me with a handful of speaking requests and my resentment boiled over. "I've written myself into a corner," I stormed. "People put me on a spiritual pedestal with a sign hanging on it, 'Don't touch.' Who enjoys pedestal-sitting? The public insists on seeing me one way when you and I know that what I really want out of life is very different. I feel trapped."

Peg was clear-eyed and unsympathetic. "You stand for something. They want to look up to you—and they want the spiritual help you can give them. What's wrong with that?"

But I found it almost impossible to get back to my work. The fact that I was in such demand as an author and a

speaker seemed meaningless. I was a forty-two-year-old
widow whom life was passing by.

Meanwhile my concern had shifted from myself to my
son's need for a father figure. So I asked for a conference
with Gordon Cosby, the young pastor of the Church of
the Saviour in Washington where I had become active. He
was the type of man in whom I found it easy to confide.

Having begun his ministry in World War II as chaplain
of the 327th Glider Regiment of the now legendary 101st
Airborne Division, Gordon had demonstrated his deeply-
felt pacifism by insisting on going unarmed into battle with
his men. In some of the hottest fighting of the War—D-
Day on the Normandy beaches, thirty-three continuous
days of fighting to capture Cherbourg, then the epic Christmas 1944 seige of McAuliffe's men at Bastogne—the chaplain simply alternated between the battlefield and the aid
station, ministering to the wounded. There with the men
of the 327th, were hammered out Gordon Cosby's convictions which later became the guiding principles of the
new church.

He brought to that church, begun in Washinton in October, 1947 a deep understanding of human weakness and
need, together with an unusual incisiveness. The church
building itself was, and still is, as unusual as its pastor.
A brownstone townhouse at 2025 Massachusetts Avenue
close to Dupont Circle was turned into a combination of
sanctuary, meeting rooms and offices.

That day in Gordon's office I confided the need I felt for
men in my son's life. "Would you keep your eyes open,"
I asked Gordon, "for men who would see this as a real
ministry for us women forced to rear sons alone? It could
take the form of going with Peter to baseball or football or

ice hockey games, or on hunting or fishing or camping trips—any such thing."

Gordon was not only sympathetic but agreed to help in any way that he could. Within the week he had located a number of men attending his church who offered to befriend the children of single parents.

A few weeks went by. Then Gordon introduced my son to Jim. He was from Wyoming, a plastics manufacturer, married, with two young children, but he had to be in Washington frequently on business matters.

Jim was a virile-looking, warm-hearted man with a good sense of humor and a fine mind. He had dabbled some in Wyoming politics at local and state levels. However, essentially he was an outdoor man who reveled in hunting and sports.

I was delighted when he invited Peter John for a two-day hunting trip or spent long hours with him in target practice. The two males seemed to enjoy each other immensely.

Then Jim began dropping by our home, and since he was there to see Peter, it seemed natural to invite him to dinner.

As time went on, Jim began asking questions about my life and activities, and I found myself responding quite openly and honestly about how lonely the life of a so-called Christian celebrity could be. He, in turn, began sharing with me some difficulties in his marriage. In the beginning, Jim's marital problems had not sounded serious; now they seemed to worsen the more he talked about them.

This should have rung alarm bells for me since I well knew that any single, unattached person of the opposite sex is not the wise choice for a marriage counselor. Instead, I would listen sympathetically, uncertain how to handle this, lulled into a false sense of security by Jim's ability to laugh at himself. That seemed to indicate at least a degree of healthy objectivity.

I will help him see how important it is for him to work out these differences with his wife, I told myself. And I did talk to him almost sternly about how important it was to get back to Wyoming and his family as soon as possible.

Then one evening after Peter had gone to his room, Jim blurted out, "Catherine, I've fallen in love with you."

A kaleidoscope of feelings swept over me: surprise, dismay, concern, fear, and yes—longing. But I knew it had to be squelched—and quickly.

"I'm startled, Jim. And—well—grateful. But it can't be right."

"I think it could be right, Catherine. But not until I'm a free man. I intend to get a divorce."

I protested and he argued. When he left that evening, I could tell that he was a very determined man.

The next morning I knew what I had to do: set the alarm, get up at 6:30 and come penitently before my Lord. With some trepidation I did this, then waited. I felt such kindness and love pouring from Him that the tears came in a flood. I knew that I had to be honest with my feelings, ruthlessly so. I poured out the residue of pain about Howard, then took pen in hand to try to analyze how I felt about Jim:

> The moments we have been together have had a special flavor, a special character. Maybe that's what often happens when one *really* lives in the present. But the companionship has the quality of something one may not keep. It's like walking through a garden and catching the whiff of a fragrance one cannot quite capture nor identify because one doesn't belong in that particular garden and can't linger there. Or hearing in the distance the haunting refrain of a melody that speaks to the heart and to the senses—but the melody must remain in the distance.
>
> Jim's friendship has done something for me. I have felt more *alive* during these days than in a long time. It's as if his touch on my life has awakened my emo-

tions, the potential warmth of me, out of a long, long sleep.

But Jim will go back to his family. He must. His friendship and companionship, the whole relationship between us, is just a loan, though a very precious one for a little time. Not the least trace of possessiveness must creep into it. I must be "hands off" in my emotional attitude towards him.

On that lofty plane I left it. But then began an insistent inner gnawing telling me that the Jim situation was unfinished business. There was a step I needed to take—a letter that would write "finis" to the whole thing. I dreaded doing it, postponed it for days. Then I forced myself to write it, stating clearly that God would never honor any relationship between Jim and me that came at the expense of his wife and children.

When I mailed the letter, it was as if I had shed a twenty-pound weight from my shoulders. The next morning I felt a surge of creative vitality I had not experienced in months. Confession and restitution had freed my spirit and out poured a torrent of words on paper:

For the past year, I have felt defeated and frustrated. And this certainly is not as God wishes it.

Here are some of the ways I have allowed my loneliness to defeat me;

1. The salt, the savor has gone out of life. Nothing, not even the very great success of *A Man Called Peter* thrills me much now. "Success" has turned to ashes in my mouth. The zest has gone out of everyday life. This is wrong. It is the outlook of a dying creature—certainly not a "new creature in Christ Jesus."

2. There has been—over the past several years—a growing coldness in my heart towards other people rather than an increasing love and warmth. Visiting the sick has been a chore—no joy in it.

3. Along with the above, there has inevitably come an increasing preoccupation with self. Or perhaps the preoccupation with self is the real cause of the defeats.

4. I have sought satisfaction in material things and have not found anything here that lasts.

5. I have become more irritable in the daily grind of everyday life. Slow drivers, inept salesgirls, parking lot attendants, provoke me much more easily than they used to.

6. I have known that God wanted me to get up an hour earlier each morning for prayer and Bible reading, yet have not been consistent about this.

7. I have failed almost totally in small disciplines of appetite—small self-denials which, at the time, I knew were right.

8. I have often failed to have the inner strength to discipline or to say "no" to Peter John, when I knew I should have.

9. Along with all these failures, I have often had a feeling of superiority to other human beings—which makes no sense at all.

I knew that the answer to this non-victorious living could be traced back to self-will. It had never been enough to go to Jesus and talk to Him about my desires and plans so that He could stamp "approved" on them. Instead, objectively, I had to seek *His* will for me in that early-morning time each day. Indeed, seek it eagerly, realizing full well that He knew what was best for me better than I knew.

In the early morning Quiet Time in my bedroom I even went back to review the Howard relationship in my Journals. I saw that what I had written seldom contained any revelations from God about whether He felt we had been right for each other. Most of my notations had amounted to wishful thinking. Too impressed with the man's stature, his appearance, his wealth, I had decided this was the one. He was not right for me—and God would have told me, had I come to Him with will and heart wide open to His counsel. Months later, viewing the relationship from God's eyes, I could easily see how mismatched we had been spiritually and emotionally.

No wonder then, the course of events with Jim had become so tangled.

Jim was not at all satisfied with my letter. He had returned to Wyoming, but then in the early fall, flew east to Washington to see me, determined to continue our relationship.

But the morning times had strengthened me and returned clear-eyedness to me. Moreover, I was learning something about how to cope with the temptations that come to the lonely: *Admit you are not able to resist on your own strength. Then step aside and let Jesus handle the situation.*

When I did this, inner direction came: *Call Gordon Cosby and meet with him.*

When I got Gordon on the phone, I hesitated only a minute. Then I told him the whole story.

"Bring Jim down here and we'll pray about it—just the three of us," he replied.

What a tremendous answer to prayer! Jim agreed to go. So we made an appointment, and I met him at the Church of the Saviour.

The moment Jim and I were seated in Gordon's study, I felt the Presence there with us. Compassionate. Approving. I could almost hear Him saying, "This is the way to handle those emotional situations that get out of hand."

Gordon listened to us without comment or change of expression. Always a creative, loving man with a pastor's warm heart, Gordon, at the same time was never afraid to use the stringent word "sin." I remembered his comments in a recent sermon to the effect that unredeemed human nature is capable of anything; that the only difference between individuals is slight variations in type and extent of sin. Then he had topped that with "The most red-blooded sinner is only capable of baby stuff compared to the manhood Christ requires of us."

"It isn't necessary for me to preach a sermon to you," Gordon told Jim and me. "You've come here because each of you wants to do what God wants you to do. I honor you both for this. Jesus always has the answer to every one of our needs."

He leaned back in his chair, smiling and relaxed. "How grateful we Christians should be! Without Jesus' agony on that cross there would be no cleansing for the likes of any of us, no miracle of changing what's wrong on the inside of us to what's right. The blood shed on that cross literally saves our lives.

"That's what the sacrament of communion should mean to us. I suggest we bring all this to the foot of Jesus' cross through communion. How about it, Jim? Are you ready to lay there your desires in this matter, what you thought was your will?"

Jim nodded, his eyes moist.

Now Gordon looked at me. "Catherine?"

"Yes, I'd like that."

The bread and the wine were there waiting on a little altar-table in Gordon's office. Never had the words been so meaningful: "This is His body broken for you..." "This is the blood of the *new* covenant, shed for many for the remission of sins. Drink ye all of it..."

We felt the Presence of Jesus in that quiet room. At the conclusion of the little service, as we knelt, Gordon blessd us both.

"Jim and Catherine, you are good friends and want to stay that way—friends. God has endowed you both with special talents and has a plan for both your lives. Jim has responsibilities to his God, his family, and his business.

God has given Catherine a son to rear and a ministry through her writing. Both need to be protected. Go your separate ways—freely forgiven, restored, refreshed, into new usefulness and creativity."

Then Gordon lifted us to our feet and hugged us both.

Several months later I heard that Jim was back with his family.

The wedding toast

X

Second Marriage

But seek first of all His Kingdom
and His righteousness
(His way of doing and being right),
and then all these things
taken together will be given
you besides.

Matthew 6:33—Amplified

Second Marriage

A strange thing happened after Gordon Cosby's communion service: I stopped thinking about remarriage. Not that the desire for it was wiped out, just that it had become much less important to me. My perspective had changed. This was the Lord's doing, of course, and came about because I was able to give the whole matter over to Him to handle.

One morning I wrote this in my Journal:

> I am to "seek the Kingdom of God first" in regard to remarriage. Should this be God's will for me, then in any given man I am to seek *first* those inner qualities of mind and heart that belong to God's kingdom.

> But what about *me*? What inner qualities should I have to qualify to be a wife again?

The next day this is what I wrote:

> Going back to the question I asked yesterday—I would list femininity, warmth of personality, vitality, interest in other people, the desire to give. A big order!

> But I am being told this morning that since it is def-
> initely God's will that I have these qualities, I am not
> to plead for them, but to believe that the prayer is al-
> ready answered, that God is giving them to me in His
> own way and in His own time.

Shortly thereafter the president of a midwestern college telephoned and asked to see me during his forthcoming trip to Washington. I had stayed at his home several years before while giving the commencement speech. Upon hearing that his wife had died, I had written him a note of sympathy.

He telephoned me upon his arrival in Washington and invited me out to dinner. By now I knew men well enough to realize that they usually ask you out for lunch if it concerns business, for dinner if it is more personal.

The college president arrived in a rented Cadillac and held my hand an extra moment when we met at the door. He was a small man, perhaps an inch or two taller than I, about fifty-five, balding, a compulsive talker. During dinner at a fine restaurant I learned everything about his college: the two million debt, the growing enrollment, the championship baseball team, the new library, the problems with some of the faculty members. But the rush of words covered up a rather surprising nervousness for a man in his position. He was obviously interested in me as a person and intended to express it before the evening was over.

He did just that, sitting in my living room later that evening. He proposed marriage. There was no attempt at any romantic buildup; it would be a marriage of convenience and mutual interest. He would supply me a home and security in return for which I would be the first lady of the college campus. I was touched and honored by his offer. But as graciously as I knew how, I refused. For me there could be no marriage without romance.

During that same year I declined two more proposals of marriage. What was happening? There could only be one answer. Relinquishment of the intense desire for re-marriage, seeking God first instead of a husband had re-laxed me in a way that was now attracting men to me. I could not analyze how I was different except that I could now empathize more with the other person and be much less concerned with myself. And the Kingdom-of-God-first yardstick was enabling me to hear the Lord's word advising me about each person.

A telephone call came one day from Leonard LeSourd, the executive editor of *Guideposts* magazine, asking for a luncheon date to talk about an idea for a future article. It had no special significance for me. I had written before for *Guideposts* and had met Len briefly one evening when I had spoken to the young adult group of the Marble Collegiate Church in New York City.

Over lunch in a Georgetown restaurant our talk ranged over many subjects. In an easy-going, personal way, Len asked many questions about me, probing, I thought, for a new subject on which to base an article. We found one, finished lunch, and he drove me home. As he stopped that car in front of my house, out of the blue came an intriguing statement, "In my twelve years at *Guideposts* I've learned a lot about the Christian faith. One aspect of it seems both bewildering and challenging."

"What is that?"

"The Holy Spirit. No one talks much about it, especially preachers. There's a mystery here—power too. Sometime I want to cover it in the magazine."

"The Holy Spirit is a He, Len," I returned quietly.

He looked at me curiously. "You know Him, then?"

"Not as much as I'd like."

The conversation ended and Len helped me out of the car and to the door. Not once during the two hours we were together did it occur to me that there was anything but a professional motive behind his invitation to lunch.

But there was nothing of the professional editor about the letter I received from Len several months later in the summer of 1959. "I would like to know you better," he wrote. "How do you react to this idea? We'll choose a day, and then you write on your calendar three letters: F U N. I'll pick you up in the morning in my car and we'll just take off to the beach or the mountains or whatever."

The letter seemed deliberately couched to say, "If you're interested in pursuing this relationship, let's have a go at it. If not, then tell me so right now."

I liked that approach. We set a day in early August. Len telephoned the night before from a Washington motel to say that he would call for me at 10:30 the next morning. He was delighted when I suggested fixing a picnic lunch.

The next morning turned out to be a beautiful summer day, not too hot. When I met Len at my front door, I found myself slipping easily into the adventurous mood he had suggested. I asked no questions about where we were going; he offered no hints. As he helped me pack the lunch into a picnic basket, I could sense his curiosity about my living situation.

"Peter John and I have lived here for several years," I volunteered, "that is, when Peter's home from Yale. This has been a good home for us, but I'm building a new house in Bethesda that will give me a better working situation.

"What's wrong with this?"

"Not enough privacy. Peter's friends are in and out a lot in the summer. I enjoy them, but there are so many other interruptions here too, and not enough space for my secretary. Anyway, I've always wanted to build my own dream house. It's already about half built."

"I see." Len was reflective. "Since Peter is at Yale nine months of the year, your dream house could end up being quite lonely for you."

"Yes—it could."

Len put the picnic lunch into the trunk of his car and we climbed into the front seat. "What do you prefer," he asked casually, "ocean or mountains?"

"I would choose the mountains."

"Which direction?"

I aimed him west toward Skyline Drive. As we drove along, I studied this fortyish editor sitting beside me. He was of medium height; dark hair beginning to grey; lithe, athletic figure. His gray-blue eyes were direct, warm, the lids often crinkling with humor. He was a good conversationalist, probing but relaxed. I relaxed too. It was going to be a good day.

While driving out Route 193 toward Route 7, we came to a sign: *Great Falls Park*.

"What's this?" Len asked.

"A scenic spot on the Potomac for picnics and walking on the rocks."

"Let's try it."

We parked, got out, and walked along the water. Since it was rocky terrain, Len reached for my hand and continued to hold it. We had lemonade at the refreshment center and then continued our drive west.

By the time we were on Skyline Drive and heading south, it was time to look for a picnic spot. Len chose a grassy knoll under a large shade tree. He took a blanket from the trunk of his car and spread it out for us to sit on. Then as I began removing the food from the picnic basket, he returned to his car trunk for another item. A ukulele!

Out of the corner of my eye as I watched Len tuning it up, I hoped that I was not about to receive a country music concert. I have nothing against country rhythms. They're fun sometimes. But on the whole, I much prefer classical music.

"I was dancing... with my darling... to the Tennessee waltz..." Len's voice had a strong nasal quality. I winced a little in spite of my effort to keep an expressionless face.

After a few bars, Len put the ukulele aside and laughed self-consciously. "You're not a country music fan, are you, Catherine? I taught myself to play—poorly, I'm afraid. And I have no singing voice. Anyhow, I'd rather talk than sing."

I sighed with relief, making a mental note that Len was perceptive, or I was very transparent—or perhaps a little of both.

It was hard to believe that two people could talk continually for eleven hours, yet feel they had scarcely made a start on subjects of mutual interest. But when Len said good-by that night, I had no real indication he could be serious about me. True, I sensed that he was surprised at certain discoveries, especially that I was not the overly-sanctimonious, lofty creature some people had painted me. We also knew now that we were both seekers, strugglers, groping towards real growth as Christians. Both of us were reporters, always interested in how to capture on paper scenes, drama, personalities, new discoveries about men in relation to God. We had an open, honest communication at a deep level.

Len's home situation however, put me on guard. For years he had been trying to rear three small children alone; he was obviously interested in finding a wife who would be willing to share this load. There was no way I could see myself in this role.

Then began frequent telephone calls. When Len invited me to come for a weekend to his little town of Carmel, New York to meet his children, to my surprise I found myself accepting. *The least I could do,* I told myself, *is to be open-minded enough to take a look at this.*

On Friday afternoon Len met me at New York's La-Guardia Airport. During the drive out to Carmel, he told me that I would meet only his two sons, Chester, six, and Jeffrey, three, that weekend. Ten-year-old Linda was at camp. Mrs. Goutremont, the elderly housekeeper, would serve as our chaperone.

The *Guideposts* property in Carmel included the magazine's business office, formerly a girl's school, and a sprawling, eight-room white clapboard house, once the home of the school president. Len and his children were living in this house set in a spacious lawn.

A picnic table had been set up outdoors under a maple tree—apparently for our supper. Diminutive Jeffrey met me with a wide smile, impish blue eyes and a hug. Chester's big, sad brown eyes stared at me suspiciously, then he held out a tentative hand. During the less-than-gourmet meal of greasy, cold fried chicken, cole slaw, potato chips, and watermelon, Chester's suspicions of me seemed to increase.

Suddenly his hand knocked over a paper cup filled with milk. Quickly I moved to one side, barely avoiding a lapful.

When Len snapped a sharp rebuke at his son, Chester flounced from the table. With the order to come and sit back down, the small brown-eyed boy fell on the ground in a wild tantrum of crying and kicking.

With a quick move, Len swept his son up in his arms, threw him over his shoulder like a sack of potatoes and carried him into the house. In a few minutes the annoyed father was back, alone.

"Chester will stay in his room until he's ready to apologize," he explained. "He seems to resent outsiders until he gets to know them, especially all women."

Jeffrey had meanwhile snuggled up close to me, obviously hungry for love. "Well, I've made one conquest anyway," I said.

"Two," replied Len with a grin.

After dinner a neighboring couple joined us for several rubbers of bridge, and I struggled to cope with three skilled players. *I'm about as adept at bridge as Len is with his ukulele,* I thought to myself.

The neighbors left, the children were asleep, Mrs. Goutremont had retired to her room. Len suggested we go outside for a walk about the grounds. It was a still, moonlit night. Suddenly his flow of talk stopped as he abruptly leaned over and gently kissed me. Then he chuckled rather self-consciously.

"We're right under Mrs. Goutremont's window, and I'll bet she's looking down at us."

I darted a quick look up at the window. It was dark. "How can you tell?"

"I can't. But she's very, very curious about us."

"Why?"

He did not answer, but instead led me to the other side of the house by the porch. Two lawn chairs were positioned there side by side, and we sat down. "I'm sorry about the episode with Chester," he began.

"It worked out fine. Your son came downstairs while you were in the kitchen and apologized. I think we're friends now."

Len sighed. "That's good. Chester looks to me for almost total security. Anyone else who visits here seems to threaten him. That has to change."

He talked about his two sons and daughter with pride. "They're such good kids. Smart too. Being without a mother the past few years has been rough. Mrs. Goutremont is the sixth housekeeper we've had."

As Len talked about his children, I saw that he had a father's heart, and I liked what I saw. He was a caring man, affectionate, comfortable to be with, mature. He approached problems calmly, I decided, thought situations through carefully, acted deliberately.

After coming to these flattering conclusions about Len, he promptly blew apart my reasoning. As he was talking about his dreams for the future, suddenly I heard him say, "and I see the two of us together."

"How do you see us?" I asked, surprised.

Even in the moonlight I could see that Len looked startled too. "I hadn't meant to go this route." He paused, struggling. "I find myself wanting to say things that will probably seem very impulsive to you. Somehow I have to—I do see the two of us together, Catherine. There's something supernatural involved in all this that I'm not sure I understand."

He stopped again and shook his head with an almost dazed expression. "I was so miserable a few months ago.

I told God I didn't see how I was going to make it alone and cried out to Him for help. Immediately after that prayer, your name, Catherine, dropped into my mind. It had to be God's doing."

"Why would you conclude that?" I queried. "I mean, why necessarily?"

"Because on my own I would never have thought you were—well, my type."

"All you knew about me came through my book about Peter Marshall?"

Len nodded. "That's mostly true. What man wants to play second fiddle to a famous Scottish preacher? Surely you must realize that *A Man Called Peter* made yours one of the great love stories of our time."

He paused, struggling for the right words. "Frankly, I thought you were too ethereal and spiritual to be any earthly good. But the Lord seemed to be telling me that I was *assuming* this about you, that I'd never really know until I investigated. So I did. That first luncheon was really an effort to probe under that professional veneer of yours. I didn't get very far that day. It was only that brief conversation we had about the Holy Spirit just before I left that kept me from forgetting the whole thing."

He reached out for my hand to cradle it in his. "All my preconceptions were exploded that day we spent together on the Skyline Drive. When I drove back to New York the next day, I kept thanking the Lord all the way home. I'm convinced He brought us together and that we are right for each other."

There was a long pause. "But I certainly hadn't intended to tip my hand so soon," he went on. "I try to approach things carefully, not blurt out my intentions like this."

I said nothing for a moment. My mind was racing furiously. *This amounts to a proposal of marriage. By making himself so vulnerable, Len is risking deep hurt.*

Finally I found my voice. "Len, you astonish me. This is only the second date we've had. How can you be so sure so soon about us? Don't you realize that with what you've just said, you've walked out on the end of a limb? The limb could so easily be chopped off. Why would you deliberately put yourself in such a position?"

"I told you—I hadn't intended saying all this. Maybe it's a deep desire for full honesty with you."

"And I honor that and respond to it. But Len, it's too soon for me to know. You're going too fast for me."

Only later did I realize... by following the dictates of his heart rather than the usual sophisticated game-playing approach, unwittingly Len had found the most direct route to my love. I felt the stirring of tenderness for him.

A few days after my return to Washington Len was back on the phone. He wanted me to come with him to Christmas Cove, Maine, for the Labor Day weekend to meet his parents. Almost wondering what would come out, I opened my mouth to reply and heard myself saying, "Yes, I could do that."

Again I flew to New York's LaGuardia Airport where Len met me. As we began the six-hour drive to Maine, Len briefed me on his parents. His father had been a Methodist minister for seven years before he had turned to education. Now he was dean of the School of Communications at Boston University. His mother, while rearing Len and his sister, Patricia, had been very active in women's clubs, Kappa Phi, church organizations.

For some time Len's parents had been conducting a yearly tour abroad and summering in Maine. From Europe his mother would bring home interesting items to stock the "Santa Claus Shop" which she had opened years before. It was a big hit with summer visitors in the Christmas Cove area.

"Mother is impressed that I am bringing you to Maine. She will want you to meet a lot of people," Len said uneasily. "I told her that we wanted to be alone to talk."

Len would be an unusual male, I thought, if he could turn off a socially-conscious mother.

We arrived at the grey-shingled LeSourd cottage on the inlet at South Bristol, Maine. The invigorating salt air brought back nostalgic memories of *Waverley*, our Cape Cod cottage. Len's parents greeted me warmly. However, the confrontation between him and his mother took place almost immediately.

"I know you said you didn't want any parties, Leonard," she began soon after we had unpacked the car, "but Mrs. Stuart insisted on having us all for a lobster dinner tomorrow night. Leonard, there simply was no way I could refuse."

"Sorry you did that, Mother," Len replied quietly. "You'll have to tell Mrs. Stuart we had already made other plans. Tomorrow night Catherine and I are going over to Boothbay."

"But, Leonard, you can go to Boothbay Sunday night."

Len shook his head. "We're going to Boothbay tomorrow night, Mother. I'll explain to Mrs. Stuart if you like. And please—no more surprises."

Mrs. LeSourd protested a little more—to no avail. Then she swallowed her disappointment as graciously as she could and made no further attempts to tie us down socially.

Len continued to be firm—to my relief. The last thing I wanted was a mother-dominated male. He kept to his plans for the two of us to be alone, to relax in the sun and talk. We started one morning while sitting on the rocks at Pemaquid Point. At three o'clock in the afternoon we suddenly realized that we had forgotten about lunch and had been in the sun too long. My legs were lobster red from sunburn.

For the next three days the almost nonstop exchange went on in cooler places. Though Len appeared to be by nature an easy-going relaxed person, he could also be determined. "We're middle-aged adults, Catherine, who have reached a point of maturity where we can make decisions more quickly," he pressed on. "I feel the Lord has brought us together; He's given me a love for you that overwhelms me, and I am ready and eager to marry you as soon as possible."

"Len, you may have your word from God, but He hasn't spoken to me yet," was my answer. "I think I'm in love with you, but I'm not yet ready to make a decision about marriage. Be patient with me."

Back in Washington after Labor Day weekend, my emotions were in a turmoil. I was facing the ultimate question: Was I going to give the rest of my life solely to a writing career—or did it also include marriage?

If I married Len I would have to move to the New York area near his work. That would mean putting my unfinished dream house on the market. I would have to leave Washington, all my friends, family and more than twenty years of memories.

One morning that still, small Voice in my inner spirit asked me some searching questions:

> You are right to be counting the cost and taking a good look at the major readjustments necessary for another marriage.

> Are there not certain areas of your life where some rigidity is creeping in? Did you not realize that My way would be to send you a man not just to satisfy your own needs of love and romance, but because he has gigantic needs himself?

Pondering this, I realized that in a first marriage, romance usually suffuses and dominates everything. It is only later, deep into marriage, that commitment to one another and the responsibilities that go along with this become as important as romance. Otherwise, the marriage has no chance of success.

But in second marriages, when we are older, commitment is writ large even at the beginning.

The question was whether I was ready for that much commitment, not just to a husband, but to three children too? Part of me was excited and stirred; the other part wanted to flee. Now I began to pray almost desperately for help and guidance.

When Len came down to Washington to meet my family and friends, Peter greeted him suspiciously at first. But I could soon tell that Len's amazing knowledge about sports was making an impression.

Len and I had dinner with my sister Em, her husband Harlow, and their two daughters, Lynn and Winifred. We drove to Evergreen Farm to meet my parents. There we also met my brother Bob, his wife Mary, and their three children, Bobby, Mary Margaret and Johnny. It was a difficult time for Len because he was put under intense scrutiny. I liked the way he handled himself: no attempt to impress, no straining for acceptance.

There were several more trips back and forth... to meet Linda, Len's ten-year-old daughter, and to talk to Norman and Ruth Peale, old friends of mine, older friends of the LeSourd family. Len had been at *Guideposts*, which the Peales had founded, for many years. Norman and Ruth confirmed all that I had heard already about him: talented editor, devoted father, spiritual seeker.

The time had come and I knew it. D-day—"Decision Day."

I was flying back to Washington from New York. As I sat in the hot, stuffy plane waiting for take-off, flocks of birds darted and wheeled beyond the edge of the runway. *Just like my darting, confused thoughts,* I mused.

The pilot's voice came over the intercom: "Sorry for the delay, folks. Things are a little stacked up here at La-Guardia this morning. Only four planes ahead of us now; maybe about fifteen minutes more."

Fifteen minutes. I did not know it then, but imbedded in those next minutes of waiting would be one shining moment that would shape the rest of my life.

As I sat buckled into my seat, I realized something: I had thought I wanted love again. But now that love was staring me in the face, I was afraid. Why did I so want to flee? What was my heart trying to tell me? Could it be because this romance was not tailor-made to my dream specifications? Len was asking me to love not only him, but to begin all over again with child-rearing. Three young children. At my age!

"Lord, You always give it to me straight," I breathed. "What am I to do?"

As I listened for His word, my mind reviewed a list of qualities that I had dreamed of in the man I wanted to marry. Basic character qualities were crucially important; others less so, like height, color of hair or eyes, whether he would be interested in yard and garden work, or a Mr. Fix-it in the house, whether he preferred loud or muted colors, or liked my favorite authors or certain beloved symphonies or piano or violin concertos. Such things I had never dared stipulate. This man, like all men, would have defects and weaknesses, just as all of us women do. Surely it is because of those human imperfections that involvement—especially in the close bond of marriage—stretches and tests us even to the point of pain.

In the past these thoughts about a second marriage had been generalities. *Now, Lord, I must focus on the particular man who has asked me to marry him. Len is offering me love that promises an end to my loneliness. I must give him an answer.*

I thought with longing of the new house being built for me in Washington, almost finished. Adjoining my bedroom, cut off from the rest of the house, would be a step-down room where I would write. It would be my sanctuary. I was most reluctant to give up all that. Still, I would live in that house alone except for those brief holiday times when my son, Peter John, would be coming back from Yale University.

Two roads stretched ahead, and I was at a crossroad. In that house being built I might produce many articles and books. There I would have a cushioned, sheltered life—yes, and probably a lonely one.

And if I chose the other road, I would plunge directly back into a turbulent life. It meant being a mother to Jeffrey, that mischievous imp of three; to Chester, six, with those enormous brown eyes and a passion for baseball; to Linda, ten, close to adolescence, and I had had no experience in rearing a daughter. I would battle to find enough time for my writing. Someone else would enjoy that beautiful, step-down room off the bedroom.

My thoughts turned again to Him: "Lord, aren't You overdoing it? Awhile back I told You that I was ready to plunge back into the mainstream of life, but does it have to be quite *this much* life? And when I thought child-rearing was over? I don't understand, don't understand at all..."

There was no immediate answer, only tumbling thoughts and question marks.

And then I remembered a sermon Peter Marshall had preached with the intriguing title "Praying Is Dangerous Business." With a clarity I would not have thought possible, several sentences came back to me:

> Perhaps you have tried to imagine in what way praying could be dangerous. Well, for one thing, it is dangerous to pray for something unless you really and truly mean it. God might call your bluff and take you up on it!

> Again, God may require something of the one who prays. The answer to our prayer may involve some real effort, maybe even some sacrifice. God's method in answering almost any prayer is the march-into-the-Red-Sea-and-it-divides method or march-right-up-to-the-walls-and-they-fall-down technique. You've got to have faith for that sort of venture and courage, too. That's why some prayers may be dangerous.

So I had prayed about remarriage, and it turned out to be one of those dangerous prayers which Peter knew so well. My bluff was indeed being called.

I took a deep breath, for there was a luminosity about this moment that I recognized. I had met it before. It had nothing to do with the other-worldly type of inspiration which many people associate with prayer and with God. It was no off-in-a-rosy-cloud vision. Actually, it was more like being slapped in the face with a wet washcloth. Or like being brought to earth with a thud and sharply bidden to stand on one's feet and behave with maturity.

Suddenly, the choice God was presenting to me was clear. To say "Yes" meant adjustment, involvement. Yet I saw that if I chose the other road, I would be turning away from the mainstream of life. That way would be comfortable, but it would take me farther and farther from contact with people. It could also mean the slow, softening deterioration of the real person inside, of the spirit God had been molding and shaping and chiseling, often so painfully.

The plane was moving now, gathering speed rapidly. We were lifting off the runway, climbing at a steep angle. The sun blazed off the silvery wings and was reflected back in pinpoints of brilliant lights.

At that instant I knew what I had to do, I would say "Yes," to life.

In deciding where we would live after our November wedding, Len and I narrowed our house-hunting down to the Chappaqua (Westchester County) area. Being considerably closer to *Guideposts'* New York editorial office than Carmel was, that would cut Len's daily commuting time.

Though these did not feature in our decision, this section held two additional pluses for me: I already had fond teen-age memories of the beautiful countryside dating back to nine weeks spent at the National Girl Scout Camp at nearby Briarcliff Manor. And Edward Kuhn, my editor at the McGraw-Hill Book Company (publisher of my books since the first one, *Mr. Jones, Meet the Master*) lived in Chappaqua. Since the relationship between author and editor is a close one (if one has the right editor), it would certainly enhance communication to be living in the same village.

With surprising ease a real estate agent helped us find the house ideally suited to our needs: a sprawling, white clapboard house with dark red shutters, three floors, 11 rooms, set in an enormous yard.

Since the house was built on a sloping lot, all of the back windows of the fully-finished ground floor looked out on the big back yard. There I would set up my hideaway workroom for writing.

As we stood hand-in-hand looking at this room, figuring out on which wall we would build bookcases, Len said, "Catherine, there are a couple of things, I—well—need to say to you. I believe that God gave you writing as your work in this world. So it's important that you keep on with that.

"And another thing—after so many years of being 'Catherine Marshall' to the public, it would be unwise and even silly for you to change your writing name at this point. I've been in the writing-editing world so long that I have no problem with it at all."

I looked at my husband-to-be, astonished and grateful. Len's face was serious, but there was a twinkle in his eyes. He meant it—and really did understand.

We were married on November 14, 1959 in the Presbyterian Church in Leesburg, Virginia, with my son, Peter, giving me away. Never have the bonds of matrimony been tied more completely by clergy: my father, a Presbyterian pastor; Len's father, a Methodist minister; and Dr. Norman Vincent Peale, a pastor to both of us, all three officiating at the ceremony, using the memorable wedding service Peter Marshall had always used, part of which he had written himself.

Linda was starry-eyed as she edged up to Peter John, her new six-foot-five brother. Chester had by now accepted me. Jeffrey, Len had decided, was too young to attend, but was eagerly waiting to see his "new mommie" again.

Early that evening after the reception at Evergreen Farm, Len and I would be flying to Los Angeles, then on to Hawaii for our honeymoon.

On our way from the church back to the farm, Len and I learned that Chester had missed seeing the ceremony. Seated beside his Grandmother LeSourd, at a moment when her attention was on the wedding service, he had slid his lithe body off the pew to the floor and mysteriously disappeared from his grandmother's grasp. Chester had spent the remainder of the service crawling under the pews from the front of the church to the back, slithering his way between the legs of the wedding guests, mopping up the floor with his best pants. At the time we laughed over the ludicrous antics of a small boy.

It should have been fair warning about what lay ahead.

Chester, Leonard, Jeffrey, Catherine, and Linda

XI

Second Family

God setteth the solitary
in families....
Beloved, let us love
one another: for love
is of God....

Psalm 68:6; I John 4:7

Second Family

❧☙

In December, 1959 upon Len's and my return from our honeymoon, I found it deeply satisfying once again to assume the role of all-out homemaker. First, there was the task of combining our possessions, deciding what to use, what to eliminate, what gaps were left to fill. The decorating job of bringing together this amalgamation was challenging and fun.

The yard dared me to make it beautiful. An outcropping of New York granite in the front yard cried out for a rock garden. A stone wall across the entire front of the property demanded a perennial border. Soon I was poring over nursery catalogues and garden books.

The children watched all this with fascination, Linda enchanted with her own room and the chance to help decide colors and other details, the boys elated over their immediate discovery of playmates next door and of so much space outdoors in which to roam.

But it takes more than a house, no matter how attractive, and possessions, and even a wonderful yard to make a home. For what is a home but people, the individuals in it, and the interaction among them?

The scene of our first dinner together as a new family is forever etched in my memory. We were gathered around the dinner table with Len's three young children: Linda, Chester and Jeffrey. My son Peter was away at Yale University.

I had lovingly prepared food I thought the children would enjoy—meat loaf, scalloped potatoes, broccoli, a green salad. Len's face was alive with happiness as he blessed the food.

But then as Chester's big brown eyes regarded the food on his plate, he grimaced, suddenly bolted from the table and fled upstairs, slamming the bedroom door behind him.

"Let him go, Catherine," Len said. Then seeing my stricken face, he explained ruefully, "I'm afraid my children aren't used to much variety in food. Mostly I've just fed them hamburgers, hot dogs, or fried chicken from a take-out place."

Len then went upstairs to persuade Chester to come back to the table. He found the little boy in bed, covers over his head, rocking back and forth. When he tearfully refused to come back downstairs, my new husband sternly told his son to undress and go to bed. There would be no supper for him. I was devastated at the thought of Chester going to sleep hungry. The dinner was spoiled for all of us.

Had Len and I but known, that scene was a harbinger of what lay ahead. Linda's resistance towards her new stepmother surfaced that first night when she refused to wear slippers on the cold hardwood floors, insisting that she had always gone barefoot around the house. I understood only too well what it must have been like to be the only female in the family. Now suddenly she was vying with me for Len's time and affection.

The two boys wanted to room together, yet were forever tussling like bear cubs. When they started scrapping yet again after lights were out, Len summarily removed Jeff to another room. The little fellow sobbed himself to sleep.

That night as I was sitting propped up in bed reading, my attention kept wandering from the child psychology book to the problems at hand. "Sibling rivalry," the learned author tagged it. "Parents, remain calm and unperturbed," his advice ran. "It happens in every family. Just remember, this too will pass."

Oh, sure, went my rebellious ruminations. *It will pass by the time parents are weary basket-cases.* I could see it so clearly: the bespectacled child psychologist before his typewriter in his cubicle of an office, the door bolted against "siblings" of all ages, cheerfully clacking out his jocular words of wisdom for us beleagured parents in the thick of it.

Later on the same night, after Len and I, exhausted, had just fallen asleep, the shrill ringing of the telephone awoke us. It was Peter. "Mom, I got picked up for speeding on the Merritt Parkway. I'm at the police station."

We agreed to post bond for Peter's release.

Yet all these troubles were but surface symptoms, the top of the iceberg of difficulties. Flooding in on us day after day were problems relating to our extended family—Len's parents and mine, along with other relatives—together with the children's emotional trauma from six housekeepers in two years. Even Peter was still suffering from his loss, shock and loneliness following his father's death ten years before.

How do you put families broken by death or divorce back together again? How can a group of individuals of diverse backgrounds, life experiences and ages ever become a family at all? I did not have the answers, but I knew Someone who did.

So I began slipping out of the bedroom at dawn while the children were asleep for a quiet time of talking-things-over prayers, Bible reading and writing down thoughts in the ever-present Journal. For example:

> Our very first step in solving family problems is res-
> olutely to view our particular difficulties as God's
> schoolroom for the truths He longs to teach us and the
> immense riches of His glory He wants to pour into our
> lives—if only we will let Him. He's going to have to be
> our Teacher all the way. What's required of us is the
> open-mindedness of the eager learner, plus taking the
> time day by day to submit practical questions to Him.

During those early morning times there dawned the realization of something I had not wanted to face: Len was
one of those men who felt that his wife was more "spiritual" than he, somehow having more Christian know-
how. Len liked to point out that I was more articulate in
prayer. Therefore, he was assuming that I would take
charge of spiritual matters in our home while he would
handle disciplining the children, finances, and such things.

I already knew from my mail how many, many women
there are who find it difficult to talk with their husbands
about anything religious, much less pray with them. How
could I make Len see that "spirituality" was as much his
responsibility as mine? *Lord, what do I do about this one?* I
hurled heavenward.

Somehow the answer was given me that nagging a male
about this would not work. My directive was to go on
morning by morning with my Quiet Time, saying nothing
about it but otherwise refusing to accept the spiritual responsibility for the home. The assurance was given me
that then God would work it out.

Meanwhile, how desperately I needed that early time
with Him! I had been transplanted from metropolitan
Washington to typical suburbia, USA. Chappaqua was and
still is a sprawling Westchester County community nick-
named "the bedroom of New York City." Every weekday
Len and most of the other Chappaqua men caught early
morning trains to the city, arriving back in the evening at

a weary 6:45—or later. During these long days, the women had to carry all family responsibilities, including seemingly endless chauffeuring of children.

A typical morning for me might go like this…A loud yelp from the boys' bedroom took me there on the run. Chester was rubbing his leg. "Jeff bit me," he grimaced. Sure enough, there were teeth marks on Chester's leg.

"You're going to be punished for this," I told Jeff sternly.

"But Chester kicked me first. Want to see where?"

I really didn't, but Jeff showed me anyway.

At that moment Linda appeared in the hallway in her night clothes, a dazed, sleepy look on her face, her feet bare. "Linda, the floor is cold. Put on your slippers."

"Can't, Mom. Can't get my feet in. The washing machine shrank them."

Obviously it was to be "one of those mornings." I went on to the kitchen to start breakfast and to fix Chester's school lunch. But I had not done my housework properly the night before: it was necessary to empty his lunch box before I could fill it. I extracted two packages of bubble gum, three rocks, a pack of well-thumbed baseball cards, and a teacher's note which he had forgotten to deliver.

The doorbell rang for a boy to hand in a special delivery letter. Then the telephone rang. Chester dripped jam on his freshly pressed school pants and had to change them. Peter, who was home between semesters at Yale, called out that he had a dental appointment in New York and that he couldn't find any clean undershorts. Linda and Chester dashed for the bus, banging the door behind them. Through the window, I saw that they *had* made it. I turned around to pour myself a second cup of coffee, and there on the kitchen counter was Chester's lunch he had forgotten to take. So-o-o, yet another errand.

I sank into the nearest chair, sorely needing that cup of coffee. As I sipped it, trying to get back some calmness and perspective, in my mind I was addressing the Almighty. *Lord, what is this about anyway? When You put people together in families, just what did You really have in mind?*

Despite myself, I could see some humor even in my previous early morning insight that God uses family problems as part of His schoolroom. "Lord, are You sure this family bit is not one of Your more sneaky tricks? I mean for hammering and chiseling and molding us into the characters You intend us to be? But You *never* give up on us, do You?"

My thoughts rambled on. Day by day I was beginning to catch glimpses of what the Creator must have had in mind by decreeing that we be born as helpless babies into the nurture of loving parents who in their turn, are required to give of themselves fully to their offspring. So the family is meant to be the training ground for life, a true microcosm for the world outside the home where person has to get along with person, pupils with each other and with teachers, employees with bosses, management with labor, nation with nation.

So how do we learn patience and tolerance and forgiveness of each other? How to stay calm and not get angry? How else except by living elbow-to-elbow in the family unit, even if there is some biting and kicking on the bedroom floor and considerable sandpapering of varying interests and personalities in the process.

I was also learning that most of us are not anything like as realistic as our God. *We* like to deal with high-flown theological abstractions. (After all, they can be kept at safe arm's length.) *He* deals with the lilies of the field, the yeast in the housewife's bread, patches on garments and curing Grandmother's arthritis. So of course the master design for us to advance toward our heavenly home via the nitty-gritty of family life would be just like Him.

Then I remembered that during His time on earth, He Himself had had to get along with at least six other children in a humble Nazareth household. What a comfort to know that He has experienced what families are up against, sympathizes, and stands waiting and available with the wisdom and help we need.

As the days went by, Len was becoming curious about why I was getting up so early. "What are you doing each morning?" he asked one day.

"Seeking God's answers for my day. I know He has them, but I have to ask Him, then give Him the chance to feed back to me His perspective and His practical helps. You see, if I don't take time for this as the kick-off of the day, He gets crowded out."

"That would be good for me, too," was Len's reaction. "After all, we're in this together. Why not set the alarm for 30 minutes earlier so that we could pray together before we start the day?"

Thus an experiment began that was to change our lives. The next day at a local hardware store I found an electric timer to plug into a small, four-cup coffee pot. That night I prepared the coffee tray at bedtime and carried it to the bedroom. The following morning we were wakened by the pleasant aroma of coffee rather than the shrill ringing of an alarm clock.

We drank our coffee, and I started to read at a spot in Philippians. But Len wanted to get on with the prayer. "You start, Catherine," he said sleepily.

"But *how* are we going to pray about this problem of Linda's lack of motivation to study?" I asked. A discussion began. It got so intense that time ran out before we got to actual prayer.

After a few mornings of this, Len agreed that we needed more time. Our wake-up hour went from 6:30 to 6 a.m. Discipline in the morning meant going to bed earlier. It became a matter of priorities. The morning time together soon changed from an experiment to a shared adventure in prayer.

By this time, Len, always methodical, had purchased himself a five-by-seven, brown loose-leaf notebook. He began jotting down the prayer requests, listing them by date. When the answers came, those too were recorded, also by date, together with how God had chosen to fill that particular need. Rapidly, the notebook was becoming a real prayer log.

Not only that, as husband and wife we had found a great way of communication. Bedtime, we had already learned, was a dangerous time to present controversial matters to one another. When we were fatigued from the wear and pressures of the day, disagreements could easily erupt.

Yet when we tackled these same topics the next morning in an atmosphere of prayer, simply asking God for His wisdom about them, controversy dissolved, with communication flowing easily between us.

Of the hundreds of entries in Len's brown notebook during this period, these were the most repeated:

1. That household help be found so that Catherine can continue the writing of her novel *Christy*.

2. That Peter will forget trying to be a playboy at Yale and find God's purpose for his life.

3. That Linda will stop rebelling against authority at home and at school.

4. That Chester will learn to control his temper and accept his new home situation.

5. That we can find the way to get Jeff out of diapers at night.

Morning by morning the requests from outside our home also piled up and up: a neighbor dying of cancer, a close friend involved in adultery, an associate with a drinking problem, parents we knew asking for advice about rebellious children, and on and on.

We were learning that specific prayer requests yield precise answers. So we did not simply ask for household help; we recorded a request for live-in help, a good cook, someone who loved children, who would be warm and comfortable to live with.

The day came when Len set down the answer to this in the brown notebook—middle-aged Lucy Arsenault. She was sent to us through Len's mother who had known her in Boston years before. Finding her enabled me actually to pick up work on *Christy* again.

I had tried to get help with Jeff's diaper problem from a highly trained pediatrician in nearby Mount Kisco. All that netted was: "Mrs. LeSourd," and the doctor's voice was tinged with sarcasm, "forget it! He'll get over it before he goes to college."

What was the point of reminding the pediatrician about the wasted time and added daily wash load of three to six diapers, plus sheets? Yet nothing we tried solved this puzzler.

That summer when we went to visit my parents at Evergreen Farm in Virginia, I felt an inner nudge to seek the homely advice of the local country practitioner. After he had heard me out, the doctor, his eyes sparkling, said, "I meet the bed-wetting problem often. I sympathize. But Catherine, you've made it too easy for Jeffrey. Nothing's wrong except that he's simply too lazy to get up and go to the bathroom, too well-padded with too many soft diapers.

"So here's the solution I suggest: waterproof the bed well. Take *all* diapers off. Steel yourself to let Jeff wallow in wet misery the rest of the night.

"But temper that with praise and reward. Put a monthly chart marked off into days on the wall by his bed. Each morning Jeff makes it dry through the night, paste a big gold star on the chart and praise him lavishly."

It worked. And we thanked God and the country doctor for his humor and common sense.

But unless we had been recording both the prayer requests and the answers with dates, we might have assumed these to be "coincidences" or just something that would have happened anyway. With those written notations marking the answers to prayer, we found our gratitude to God mounting. The prayer log was a marvelous stimulus to faith.

Len and I were certainly being taught about prayer as we submitted the practicalities of daily life to God. Yet not all prayers were answered the way we had anticipated. We found that prayer is not handing God a want-list and then having beautiful answers float down on rosy clouds. Also, His timing is certainly not ours; most answers came more slowly than we wished, and piecemeal.

Those answers were also presented to us not simply through some change in external circumstances, but just as often through inner guidance. That meant that what God had to say to us in our early morning times was even more important than what we presented to Him.

Out of His direction came some household rules:

1. Meals at regular hours and at least the evening meal eaten together as a family unit whenever possible. Dinner thus to be the focal point of each day.
   (Each child soon learned to say a grace, was encouraged to articulate personal thoughts and needs, and to participate in the discussion of current events. At the end of the meal Len or I read something from the Bible and then closed with prayer, again with each child participating, if only one sentence.)

2. Regular bedtime, though later on weekends.

3. No television for children on school nights. TV and movies on weekends to be screened carefully.

4. Linda's endless telephone conversations with friends to be limited to one period, 3:30 to 6 each afternoon. No twosome dates until she is 16.

5. Time to be given to the children on weekends for family outings and/or home games. (We kept a bulging closet of games.)

6. On Sundays go as a family to church.

7. Len and I to share checking on children's school homework. Our full interest and participation in the Parent-Teacher Association and all school events pertaining to our three.

(Though we would listen carefully to our children's complaints and be fair, we stressed that the teacher's and principal's authority would always be upheld.)

8. Discipline always to be part of our life together; punishment to fit the disobedience; spankings (administered by Len) by no means ruled out.

The implementation of all this was never easy. In the seventh grade, Linda was bright and freckle-faced with all the instincts of a tragic actress. Like all her peers, she was trying to grow up too soon. Len and I became accustomed to the cry, "Oh, you just don't understand-d-d."

Naturally, the majority of our notations in the prayer log focused on our children during those early years. In rearing them, we were gradually learning that God was more interested in our learning the patience to wait for *His* answer to particular problems than in our painfully learning the hard way by rushing ahead of Him trying out schemes *we* had devised.

Patience? What could be better calculated to teach patience than trying to drum manners and tidiness into children? Before dinner on three nights out of five: "Boys, you call *those* hands clean? Back to the bathroom you go..." "Jeff, elbows off the table." "Chester, it's no good trying to hide the carrots under the lettuce leaf..." From Len, "Linda, are you trying to use your *hair* for dental floss? *Take your hair out of your mouth.*"

Or, "For the 687th time, who left towels on the bathroom floor this time?"..."Boys, this room is a mess. Get those clothes off the floor and hang them up."... "Linda, I've asked you over and over *not* to doodle on the wall while you're on the telephone...." Surely the writer of that Holy Writ, "Let patience have her perfect work" must have had parents in mind.

Or consider Jesus' admonition that we forgive seventy times seven. Perhaps Christ was not thinking specifically of the family unit when He spoke those words, or I think He might have trebled the figure.

How to get practice in forgiveness? There was the matter of Jeffrey repeatedly leaving ink cartridges in his pants pocket and in that way ruining an entire tub of laundry. Each time I put away the family wash, every white garment had the navy-blue measles. Forgiveness. Forgiveness!

Then there was Chester's habit of forgetting everything because his mind was floating around somewhere on cloud nine. He could not wear his P.F. Flyers because he had left them at the public tennis courts; his sweater was abandoned at Donn's house; it was impossible to do his assignment because he had left his book at school. As I would step on the accelerator for those time-consuming trips to the tennis courts and to Donn's house to collect possessions, I knew that I must find the way "not to let the sun go down on my wrath."

Or late one afternoon I glanced out one of the front windows and did a double-take at Linda kneeling in the newly planted rock garden. My mind refused to believe what my eyes were seeing. Carefully, methodically, she was dragging, first on one side, then the other, newly purchased white sneakers through the garden dirt. My indignant protest brought only a withering, "Mom, *everyone* wears dirty sneakers. I'd just look crazy if mine were all new and white."

And there was Jeffrey's strange fascination with, of all things, shoelaces. One morning in nursery school the teacher asked him to stand up and recite. Jeff tried hard to struggle to his feet, he really did. But how could a guy straighten up when he had tied the laces of his Keds securely to his belt?

Then there was the afternoon I put him down for a nap. In no time disconsolate crying was issuing from the bedroom. I found Jeff trapped under the bed, his shoelaces woven in and out of the bedsprings, knotted over and over.

Or after he had learned to read: "Jeff, no wonder you're so irritable this morning. You sneaked reading again last night, didn't you?"

"Well..." The look was downcast.

"No use denying it. I found *The Secret of Fiery Gorge* shoved under your bed.

But Jeff liked to fight with his back to the wall. "But Mom, how could I have read? Bet you didn't see my light on."

"No. But you read anyway. And I know how."

The blue eyes searched me suspiciously, only half believing. "How *could* you know?"

"Special radar."

This was too much. Now he must know. "How? Tell me how then."

"By lying on the floor by the door with the book tilted to catch the light from the hall, that's how."

Jeff looked at me, all his impishness showing. "Gee, Mom, I wish I had a *dumber* Mother!"

Through all this we learned that even though children resist discipline, all of them crave the security of firm structure and are confused and rudderless when parents give in to them out of fear of their own offsprings' displeasure. Years later our children would be admitting that secretly they had been relieved at the way we had stood our ground with them.

As an older girl, Linda would often comment, "I feel sorry for poor so-and-so. She can do anything she wants to do. I think her parents just don't *care*."

As time went on, an especially significant answer to prayer was unfolding before me, my plea that Len would assume his proper role as the spiritual head of our home.

His first insight was the realization that the two boys were going to pattern almost everything after him. This was so obvious with something like athletics. Len had begun teaching his sons to swing a baseball bat as soon as they could lift it. He pored over the newspaper sports pages each morning. As soon as Chester and Jeff could read, they too were studying the sports pages.

If the Christian faith was to become important to them, it would happen through their father. Otherwise the two boys would conclude that religion was for the womenfolk and ignore it. With this revelation, Len did an about-face on turning spiritual matters over to me; he became the one to call the family together for prayer around the table.

As the boys witnessed their father spontaneously praying and were called on to follow, they were soon responding, praying aloud with no self-consciousness.

One evening we went to dinner at a crowded restaurant. I had just picked up my fork when Chester quietly remarked, "In school today our teacher was talking about saying grace before meals. He said that we should not skip doing this even when we're eating out."

There was a pause during which Len and I looked at one another. Len nodded in agreement. "Your teacher was absolutely right, Chester. We should have done that all along."

Around the table we inclined our heads slightly. In a low-keyed voice Len thanked God for the food. Jeff's chatter started as soon as the soft "Amen" was out of his father's mouth. We thought that we had been exceptionally unobtrusive in the crowded dining room.

But when the meal was almost over a nice-looking young

man approached Len, leaned over, spoke several sentences for his ear alone, smiled, and left.

"What was that all about?" I asked curiously.

Len was looking bemused. "The man wanted me to know that he thought it was great for a family not to be ashamed to pray in public. I feel I've been given credit for something I don't deserve."

So part of the beautiful answer to this prayer, I sat there thinking, is that Len himself does not realize *how far* he's come. As he became the spiritual head of the household, I was given the freedom to play the supporting role as I had in my marriage to Peter. In no way did I consider this a secondary role. Len and I continued as a team, checking and sometimes correcting each other. Household help freed me to write in the mornings, leaving afternoons and evenings for family matters.

After five years in Chappaqua the cold New York winters were handing me frequent colds, all too often ending in protracted bouts of bronchitis. The doctors advised a warmer climate for me.

Len dispatched me to Florida to investigate rentals for the four-month winter season of 1964-65. We ended up buying a house in Boynton Beach and moving there in November, 1964 since Len discovered he could still handle his editorial responsibilites at *Guideposts* while commuting back and forth between Florida and New York City.

The two boys quickly adjusted to the change of location. Linda, however, was finding life more difficult as she entered a stage of adolescent rebellion against her parents. There were occasions when I felt close to this gifted but often troubled girl, more times when I felt like a rejected parent. I struggled with all of the negative stepmother images. Often I caught myself resenting this child and her attitudes. Since this was not my image of the "good mother," I tried to ignore or bury such emotions.

When we were still living in Chappaqua, I would seek God's help for this in my Quiet Times. He met me one Sunday in church. The winter sunlight was streaming in the tall arched windows laying long patterns of light across the white colonial sanctuary. I was sitting there thinking about Linda. Suddenly in my mind and heart His voice was speaking to me with particular clarity and intensity. *Unless you love her, you don't love Me.*

Lord, I know that's true. The thought stabbed me. *But how do we love certain persons when we hate some of the things they do? Please tell me how. And Lord, I have another problem. I can't manufacture love. Nobody can. How can I manage it unless You give me that love as a sheer gift?*

With the issues thus clearly drawn, I struggled on. Over and over I would take a fresh grip on my willingness to love Linda no matter what she did—all the way from minor infractions to slipping out of her bedroom window after midnight for a date with a senior football star five years older than she. Or an ostensible trip to the library being rather a rendezvous with a boy in the village. Since we did not want her to date until she was 16, she showed us how many devious ways there were around that rule.

As I willed to love, I asked God to take care of my emotions and make my love real. For a time it would work, and our home would know contentment and harmony. Then another crisis would develop and I would fall on my face.

The difficulties grew until Linda was finding life all but unmanageable. For years, schoolwork had been difficult. Here was a bright girl whose grades seesawed wildly between "A" and flunking. Almost every term report carried teachers' comments about "poor attitude and motivation" and "work not up to level of ability." Tutors and extra sessions and finally, a preparatory school brought no demonstrable results.

During these years, both in Chappaqua and in Florida, her father and I had tried everything we knew—guidance counselors, a child psychologist, counseling with Christian friends, group prayer, prayer at Linda's bedside while she was asleep—every type of prayer we could think of. There had been some breakthroughs, such as the times she came home from prep school and really participated in our family devotions. Even so, Len and I knew that the root problem remained. It seemed to be centered in her will; she appeared to be unable to want to be any different.

In college the trouble grew. To academic difficulties was now added the youth revolution of the late 1960s. Linda plunged wholeheartedly into it: life pattern, clothing styles, long straight hair, wire-rimmed spectacles, protest meetings, campus sit-ins, hitchhiking to peace marches and rallies, one of them all the way from the city of Delaware, Ohio to Washington, D.C.

Graduation from college came for our daughter in June, 1971. Linda's father, grandparents, and I arrived at the graduation scene to find a very unhappy girl on our hands. There was a thin veneer of normality, but flashes of irritation and anger kept breaking through to us. The strain in the relationship between Linda and me was obvious, her dissatisfactions deep.

Watching the academic procession walk by on sneakers or T-thong sandals, with mortarboard caps tilted on the heads at every possible angle, I wondered what the other graduates were feeling. Were most of them malcontents too, with life somehow out of kilter, values all a-jumble?

The scene left me with such heaviness of spirit that after our return home I spent one morning working on the release of all my resentments against Linda stretching back over the years to age ten. To my astonishment, I filled three pages.

Though I found it difficult to show this list to Len, I felt the need of such "walking in the light" as a step towards cleansing. Certainly Jesus had made it clear that our harboring any resentment is a sin needing the Father's forgiveness. Not only that, a sin carrying a dreadful penalty:

> And whenever you stand praying, forgive, if you have anything against any one; so that your Father also who is in heaven may forgive you your trespasses.[1]

With the list before us, Len and I prayed about this together. First, my confession of these resentments followed by the claiming of His glorious promise of immediate forgiveness.

Yet I well knew that resentments are emotions so deeply imbedded that we cannot shed them by a shrugged-off wishing them away. How great then to know that as we set the rudder of our wills to forgive and tell God so, *He* will undertake for us the task of untangling and cleansing at the emotional level.

At that point I got a fresh view of the meaning of the Cross. Our resurrected Lord stands before us, nail-pierced hands outstretched, saying, "Hand Me your resentments, your grudges, your anger. *All* of it. *That's* what I died for. As you decide in your will to hand Me all these negatives and tell Me so, I still, in the present, literally absorb these negatives into My own body. Even as the corruption of death was transmited into Life in My resurrection body, so in exchange for your sin I hand you My love—freely, abundantly enough to over-flow to the very one you have resented."

So, I thought wonderingly, then the exchange made possible by Jesus' Cross—His love and new life in return for my sins—was not just something that happened at a point in time, historically. That atoning work is still going on.

This shed new light on the Apostle Peter's words:

He personally bore our sins in His (own) body to the
tree... that we might die... to sin and live to righteousness. By His wounds you have been healed.[2]

Neither Len nor I told Linda anything about our prayer
of release. We did not have long to wait to see results.

Several weeks later on Cape Cod during that tumultuous
summer of 1971 came the climax to our long years of struggle with this particular situation. When my grandchild,
Amy Catherine Marshall, was born on July 22 with severe
liver, kidney and brain damage—a group of us gathered
on the Cape for concentrated prayer.[3] On an impulse I
telephoned Linda, who was working in her grandmother's
Santa Claus Shop in Maine. Would she care to join us?

There was a moment's silence. "Yes," she said, "I'd like
to be there."

Afterward, Linda told me that she wanted to come because I was the one who had telephoned and invited her.
What happened when she got there literally reversed the
direction of Linda's life. As is usually the case, people
other than her parents—Len and me—were used by God
as the catalyst for our daughter. The turning point that
followed is best told in her words...

On the afternoon after my arrival at Cape Cod I was
about to take a shower. A particular moment is crys-
tallized forever for me. I had one foot on the bathroom
rug, the other in the shower stall. At that instant, like
a bolt, the realization hit me that one foot in, one foot
out was an accurate representation of my life so far.
Several times I'd gone through the motions of com-
mitting my life to God. Yet I did not have an obedient
heart. I was living in outright rebellion against Him.

I sensed that this was the moment to decide—for
Him or against Him. There could no longer be any
middle ground.

Standing there, I carefully weighed what choosing
the Lord's side would cost me. Obviously, some things

in my life would have to go. But I was tired of living in two worlds and not enjoying either. Desperately, I longed for His peace in my heart. I took a deep breath and said aloud, "I choose You, Lord." Then I got in the shower. That shower was my true baptism.

The following day came many hours of agonizingly honest dialogue with Len and me. Tears flowed. After that I understood why the direction given me in the Chappaqua church—*Unless you love her, you don't love Me*—had been so difficult for me.

"I thought I wanted a loving relationship with you when you married Dad," Linda told me. "But resentment crowded in. The reason was that at a gut level I thought you were taking Dad away from me. I would no longer be number one in his life."

During this long evening of honesty and confession among the three of us and then to God in prayer, many barriers came crashing down. For Linda it was the release of years of hostility and guilt. For us, it was a facing up to mistakes and fears and lack of understanding.

Following this, it was Linda herself who wanted to crown all these events with a "believer's baptism" in the ocean followed by a communion service on the beach.

That was not the finish of this particular episode. For God had some further work to do in me the morning after the communion service.

During the intervening hours, my mind must have flicked at some secret thoughts along the line, "All those years of agony she put her father and me through, then she's forgiven by God *instantly*. Isn't that too easy a forgiveness?" Ugly secret thoughts—except God knew.

The next morning I was awakened to the clear, incisive internal message, "Remember My story of the prodigal son? You're in grave danger of taking the place of that elder brother. That morning you didn't quite mean business about finally releasing all those 'aughts' against Linda, did you? I heard and answered anyway. *Now let them go.* For now, take the lowest seat at My banquet table, below Linda. And I want you to confess all this to Linda this morning."

Thus I was properly zapped, as our boys would say. Humbly and a trifle haltingly, at breakfast I made my confession to Linda. She wept again, this time for joy, then ecstatically hugged me. It was a reconciliation written in heaven.

And so Len and I have grown over the years as parents, and our morning time together has set the tone and direction of over 21 years of marriage. That original coffee-timer (still operating, although with many new parts) is one of our most cherished possessions. We know that neither one of us, or both of us, without God have the wisdom to handle the problems which life hands us day by day. But as early morning prayer partners we have added assurance that "where two or three are gathered together" in His name, our all-loving and all-wise Saviour, Rescuer, and Lord is indeed with us.

Four generations , Leonora , Catherine, Edith and Mary Elizabeth

XII

Grandmother

And all thy children
shall be taught of the Lord;
and great shall be the peace
of thy children....
The Lord shall bless thee....
(and) thou shalt see thy
children's children....

Isaiah 54:13; Psalm 128:5,6

Grandmother

A never-ending source of wonder to me is the way God continues to reveal new truth to His children, especially to those who reach an age when they think they know a few things about the Christian faith. As the years went on, I thought, *Surely now in my latter years I'll be able to put to good use what wisdom I have accumulated.* Instead, I have been going through one of the most intense learning periods of my life. Especially in connection with our children and grandchildren.

Peter John graduated from Yale in rebellion against a God who had taken his father away by death. During one of our morning prayer times, Len received the guidance that he was to encourage Peter to attend a conference of the Fellowship of Christian Athletes at Estes Park, Colorado. Peter surprised us by deciding to go. There he was challenged by his huddle leader, Donn Moomaw, a former all-American football player, now a Presbyterian pastor. When Donn bluntly told Peter that he was fleeing God and messing up his life, Peter was so convicted that by the end of the conference he had made a commitment to Jesus Christ. Len and I stood by almost as spectators and watched as amazing changes took place in Peter.

First, he enrolled at Princeton Theological Seminary within a month after his experience at Estes Park. There he began attending a prayer group composed of students who had experienced an infilling of the Holy Spirit. To the uneasiness of seminary authorities, the students were manifesting some of the gifts of the Spirit in these meetings. Healings were taking place, damaged relationships were being restored. A new movement of the Holy Spirit was moving among the seminarians.

When Peter next came home on vacation, he challenged Len and me about our openness to the Holy Spirit. Had we been baptized with the Spirit? If not, how could we really hope to make any progress in the Christian Life?

As he talked, I thought back, remembering that summer of 1944 when I had found myself with such intense curiosity about the Holy Sprit; how this had resulted in a careful study of the Old and New Testaments, ending with a quiet asking for this Gift of all gifts. But Peter was still not satisfied. Then why, he questioned, was I not manifesting some of the *particular* gifts of the Spirit?

Stunned by the 180-degree change of direction in my son, here is a notation I made at the time:

> When Peter graduated from Yale, he informed us that he might decide to be a beach boy at Virginia Beach for awhile. Now he is deep into the Holy Spirit movement. What is going on, Lord? We prayed that Peter would find You in his own way, and this has been gloriously answered. But now I must look deeply into this somewhat strange but exciting new contemporary activity.

Len and I had already become interested in this movement through our editorial relationship with John and Elizabeth Sherrill. While writing *The Cross and the Switchblade* with David Wilkerson, the Sherrills had had an experience with the Holy Spirit, resulting in some momentous changes in their lives. The impact of all this on Len and me was to bear lasting fruit in our lives.

Then Peter announced to us that he thought he had found *the* girl, a fellow-student at Princeton Seminary, the daughter of Dr. and Mrs. Calvin Wallis, medical missionaries to Guatemala. One weekend he brought her home to Chappaqua.

Edith Wallis was tall, blonde—a joyous creature—and a real answer to prayer.

Before Peter was in his teens I had begun praying for my son's future mate, wherever she might be. As I continued praying, I had asked myself, *What would be the characteristics of spirit and mind and heart of that "just right girl" for my son*? I was not so much concerned with whether she would be a blonde or brunette; surely the inner beauty would dictate the outer.

Being me, I took pencil in hand and committed to paper, item by item, the lineaments of my dream girl. Most important of all, this girl would have met Jesus Christ for herself and would have fallen in love with Him. She would have a good mind, with enough education for mutual, intellectual stimulation. She would have a lot of the joy of life in her, a sense of humor, a certain zing—and so on and on.

Then when the portrait seemed complete, one morning I placed the dream in God's keeping, asking Him to correct any flaws in it and bring it into fruition in Peter's life in His own time and His own way. I stuck the note about my dream girl between the pages of an old Bible and forgot about the paperwork on it.

Ten years later, as I was dusting and rearranging a shelf of books one morning, the slip of paper fell out of the old Bible. I read it, astonished. Here was a perfect description of Edith Wallis. God had thrown in a few extra goodies as dividends. She was tall like Peter, blonde like Peter, a wonderful cook—what man wouldn't like that! She was interested in gardening like Peter. And I loved her immediately and have never stopped thanking God for such a momentous answer to prayer.

Peter and Edith determined that their wedding must be in keeping with their Christian commitment. Three ministers would take part, which reminded Len and me of our wedding. There would be congregational singing and a sermon, features rarely included at that time. Moreover, the elders of the Rye Presbyterian Church, where the service was to be held, would administer the sacrament of the Lord's Supper not only to the bride and groom as the first act of their married life, but also to the entire congregation. As it turned out, this unusual wedding lasted one hour, twenty minutes.

Naturally there were some cautious comments afterward about the uniqueness of the wedding—all the way from, "Well, we've never seen a couple married so thoroughly," to "I've never been so touched by the sincerity of two young people," to "I couldn't help wondering what So-and-So thought about a *sermon* at a wedding!"

But Len and I noticed that to 16-year-old Linda especially, it was everything a wedding should be. She had glimpsed true romance, had seen it in front of the altar being dedicated to God. There were stars even in her still rebellious, nonreligious eyes. "It was the greatest wedding ever!" she exulted.

Fifteen years later we were to see the significance of Linda's reaction.

After graduation from Princeton Seminary, Peter's first

charge was as an assistant pastor in West Hartford, Connecticut.

Then in early May, 1967 Edith and Peter gave us the exciting news that they were expecting their first child.

Peter telephone me on December 3, 1967. "It's a boy, Mom." But his voice was not as excited as a man's should be over his first child. Then it came. "Something's wrong, Mom. 'Poor muscle tone,' the doctors say."

Lung congestion followed, the threat of pneumonia. That Sunday Peter crawled in under the oxygen tent to christen the baby Peter Christopher—"Christ-bearer."

I wanted to come at once, but the new parents urged me to wait. Days dragged by with the baby still in the hospital. Early one morning during a time of prayer, I was told that now the time had come to fly north. This was followed by the rather surprising instruction, "Go—and crown my prince with thanksgiving."

The next day I began the journey to West Hartford. During a seemingly interminable three-and-a-half hour wait at New York's Kennedy Airport, a heaviness of spirit alerted me. There must be some crisis involving the baby.

Later I found out. During my delay at Kennedy, Peter Christopher had stopped breathing, had turned blue, then stony white. The loving hands of friends had been laid on the baby in prayer and miraculously, he had begun to breathe again.

But not for long.

The first glimpse of my new grandson was of a pink and normal looking baby, his perfect round head promising blonde hair. Memories came flooding back. The baby looked exactly as his father had as a new-born.

I so yearned to cuddle my grandson. But I had my instructions, "Go—and crown my prince with thanksgiving."

It was easy—and hard. Easy because Peter Christopher was such a perfectly formed baby with a gentle spirit felt by all of us. Hard to crown God's little prince with *thanksgiving* if he was about to be taken from us.

With Peter and Edith standing by the crib and the doctor and some nurses looking on from a discreet distance, gently I laid my hands on the soft skin of that little head. "You gave him, Lord. He is Your prince, You told me. We hereby, according to Your instruction, crown Peter Christopher with thanksgiving, the golden crown of gratitude for this life You have given."

Thirty-five minutes later, the young doctor sadly informed us, "He is gone." It was almost as if that gentle spirit had been hanging on until I got there to bestow the blessing.

As all of us present tried to minister to Peter and Edith, I struggled with my own emotions. *Lord, I don't understand. When Peter Marshall died, Your sure word to me was that "goodness and mercy" would follow me all the days of my life. Lord, is this goodness and mercy?*

I looked at Edith, her face wet with tears. Edith, born to be a mother. *What about it, Lord? Is Edith then, not to know the joy of motherhood? And am I then not to be a grandmother?*

The Lord's answer to this questioning came two and a half years later with the birth of Mary Elizabeth Marshall, a healthy baby with perfect muscle tone. "Thank you, Lord. Forgive me for my doubts." In my rejoicing over this new life, I pushed down deep inside me the unresolved questions with which I had been wrestling.

I loved being a grandmother. Not since I was a small girl had I had so much fun. Not only that, I learned volumes about the delight of living in the Kingdom of God while still on this earth.

As a tiny girl Mary Elizabeth had large, round blue eyes and a piquant nose framed by blonde hair like her mother's. By the time she could walk, she had sturdy, well-formed legs that carried her into the most unlikely places, a disarming smile with a touch of coyness, and a way of pronouncing "Yes" and "Oh, no—no—*no*" that made her sound like a charter member of the Women's Liberation Movement.

When this child visited us what she did to our household was remarkable. My writing schedule was forgotten while Mary Elizabeth and I would enjoy a tea party using tiny blue cups which I had carted from Salzburg, Austria, in anticipation of such a golden moment. Our son Jeffrey had no objection to becoming a baby tender. He never walked Mary Elizabeth around the block in her stroller; he raced her while she chortled. And when she flirted with her grandfather, Len would become so entranced he would drop down on all fours, bray like a donkey and kick his heels in the air.

All of this added up to joy. We watched Mary Elizabeth awaken each morning to a world full of wonders. What had become commonplace to us jaded adults still had the freshness of surprise for her. The flying birds, the cloud formations, cows seen in a field, a flower, fragrances, food over which to smack the lips, the rhythm of nursery rhymes and poetry, music—all filled her with excitment.

And like any normal child, she had that wonderful God-given gift of living in the present and expressing what she felt immediately, exuberantly, without self-consciousness.

She shared this gift with us almost from the beginning. One such memory: On the patio of our home in Florida we were celebrating Mary Elizabeth's second birthday. The candles had been blown out on the cake gaily decorated with circus animals. The ice cream had been eaten. Finally, it was time to open the gifts. Adult hands helped Mary Elizabeth open a box almost as big as she was. The last bit of tissue paper was lifted off and out of the box came the

little girl doll "Puddin'." Joy, glee, exultation chased themselves across my granddaughter's face. She clasped her
hands, then reached for "Puddin'," hugged her to herself,
chortled, cried for joy, gasped, shouted. No present ever
hit the mark so surely. Every female atom in the little girl
was focused on the doll with an intensity of awareness.

From that moment, "Puddin'" became Mary Elizabeth's
love and has remained so through ten years, two new
wigs, arm and leg replacements, and twenty other rival
dolls of all sizes and types.

But the moment was also a gift for us who watched, the
gift of a memory to enjoy over and over.

Through adventures like this with our granddaughter,
the rest of us were reminded of Christ's extraordinary
statement, "Except ye become as little children, ye shall
not enter into the kingdom of heaven." We began to understand why Jesus was careful to specify the diminutive
"little children." These very tiny ones are still fresh from
the hand of their Maker, children who have not yet had
time to absorb the prejudices, the resentments, the social
distinctions and cruelties, the conflicts and repressions
which we grown-ups mistakenly call "wisdom."

In my reading recently, I came across descriptions of
how adults feel when they enter the Kingdom of God
through what Jesus called "the new birth." Interestingly,
what they experience is almost identical with what we
watched in Mary Elizabeth. This is how one woman de-
scribes it:

> "I cannot say exactly what the mysterious change
> was. I saw no new thing, but I saw all the usual things
> in a miraculous new light, in what I believe is their true
> light.
>
> Every human being, every sparrow that flew, every
> branch tossing in the wind, was caught in and was a
> part of the whole mad ecstasy of loveliness, of joy, of
> importance, of intoxication of life..."[1]

It made me think of Mary Elizabeth's father at age five, standing with his nose pressed against the windowpane, laughing with glee at the fireworks of an autumn thunder storm. "Mommy," he told me, "the lightning looks like string beans dancing." They did indeed, but my prosaic adult mind would never have caught such an analogy.

Another aspect of this springtime of life—almost as if small children were back in the Garden of Eden—is that Mary Elizabeth felt the necessity of naming every living creature around her. She was not really at home during her first visit to our new Florida setting until she had decided upon names acceptable to her. Thus Mary, who helps us keep house, became "Yehh-yehh"—usually enunciated as lustily as if Mary Elizabeth were rooting for the Braves. Great-grandmother was tagged "Na-na." Len was "Popi." By Christmas time, Mary Elizabeth could manage "My-grandma," but "Jesus" was impossible, so He became the "Baby Zoohpff." I believe that He heartily approved.

Oddly this naming task was one of the first functions that God gave to the original man Adam: "... the Lord God formed every beast of the field and every bird of the air, and brought them to the man to see what he would call them..."[2]

I had often wondered why the writer of Genesis brought in this specific detail. Mary Elizabeth showed me why. God loves *all* of His creation. Whatever He made He saw that "it was good." So the name is just one indication of how special, how cherished all of us and the beautiful world in which He set man, are to Him. In the Kingdom of God, His love is all inclusive, from a bug crawling on the floor, to a butterfly floating over the flowers, to all animals, to each one of us.

And in the Kingdom of God the heart is tender. We grown-ups have only to watch little children to realize how calloused we have become. Among Mary Elizabeth's fa-

vorite books was one of the nursery rhymes set to music.
The first time her mother sang to her

> "Rock-a-bye baby in the treetop
> When the wind blows the cradle will rock,
> When the bough breaks the cradle will fall
> And down will come baby, cradle and all"

Edith was startled to have her daughter burst into tears.
Then she understood: Mary Elizabeth was crying because
the baby had fallen down. Since the tears were genuine,
Edith made up a story about how Daddy had come and
picked up the baby, kissed her, and had found that the
baby was not really hurt at all. That comforted Mary Elizabeth temporarily. But from that day on, whenever she
came to that page in the book, there was a loud "No!" as
she flipped over the page.

Watching all this, we could but conclude that the little
child has no problem about belief in God. These small ones
are still living on the borderline of two worlds. "Train up
a child in the way he should go and when he is old, he
will not depart from it" goes the old proverb. Since Jesus
said, "*I* am the way," I am grateful that from the beginning
our granddaughter was taught about Him. She did not
feel comfortable about going to sleep at night until she had
shut her eyes tightly, held hands with whoever was putting her to bed and said a happy good-night to the "Baby
Zoohpff".

In November, 1967 Peter accepted a call to the First
Wesleyan Community Church in East Dennis, Massachusetts. Then on July 22, 1971 a third child was born to Peter
and Edith. It was apparent from her birth that Amy Catherine had suffered severe damage to internal organs. By
now the doctors were calling it "genetic aberration cerebro-

hepato-renal syndrome." Medically speaking, they gave no hope. Of some forty-odd cases recorded, all had died within about six months.

Those of us on the scene felt called to pray in total faith, asking for a miraculous healing. We were joined by Peter's congregation, by ten close friends who flew to the Cape to join us for intensive prayer, and by many, many others. If ever a family went out on the end of a limb of faith, we did. As for me, not since Peter Marshall's first heart attack had I thrown everything I am and have, every resource of spirit and mind and will, into the battle for a human life.

Meanwhile, in the space of a few days those who had gathered on the Cape were seeing extraordinary answers to prayer: Jamie Buckingham, one of the group, prayed for a friend's granddaughter, eight-year-old Amy, on the same floor with Amy Catherine at Boston Children's Hospital. The little girl had cystic fibrosis. One lung had been removed, infection had set in, and Amy was dying. Later we found that the child's miraculous recovery had begun that day. Her grandmother later reported, "Amy is now in full health, attending school in Connecticut."

There were miracles of a different kind too. Our daughter Linda experienced a complete reordering of her life, lifting her out of darkness and confusion into a new beginning; a man's resentment against his father, festering since childhood, was healed; our friend Virginia Lively was given the key to her daughter's health, an answer she had been seeking for a long time; a floundering marriage was made right again. It was as if tiny Amy had become a divine catalyst, calling forth a concentration of God's power and love.

When our friends had to depart after three days, I moved to Children's Inn near the hospital in Boston, while Peter and Edith took turns keeping vigil over Amy and driving back and forth to Cape Cod to be with Mary Elizabeth. Day after day we sat beside the baby who was stretched out on a slanting "heat bed" under a big light. Was not the light, I wondered, agony for the sensitive eyes of a new-born? And Amy was hungry. She would open her mouth expectantly like a baby bird, yet was unable to suck; she had to be fed intravenously, the seemingly endless tubes sticking out in all directions.

She needs to feel loving arms, my heart kept telling me. Finally, the nurses assented and one morning they carefully placed her in my arms, tubes and all. She cuddled up, nuzzling me, seemed more alert. With this much encouraging response, we decided to increase our vigil to an around-the-clock one, so that Amy could have some cuddling even during the night. It was apparent that this baby's spirit was different from the gentleness we had felt in Peter Christopher. It was as if he had been a small angel who had briefly brushed life on earth, while Amy was a fighter who wanted to live.

Nonetheless, on the morning of September 4, as I was holding the baby, she began to have difficulty in breathing. A few minutes later Amy's heart stopped beating. Her time on earth had been but six weeks.

As it had at Peter Christopher's death, the agony returned to my spirit. The taking of Amy Catherine devastated me even more than that of Peter Christopher; it went deeper because now it had happened twice.

I wrote in my Journal

> My heart, my whole being has been acting out 'Rachel weeping for her children and would not be comforted because they were not.' (After Herod's slaughter of the innocents.)

> An unexpected revelation is how slight the difference is between the feelings of a mother and a grandmother. Scarcely a hair's breadth! I had not anticipated this. I could not have been more acutely sensitive to Amy and her plight had I borne her in my own body. . .

During the next few months I experienced the most intense misery I have ever known. Life went gray. Nor was it all psychological or spiritual. Events in the professional world began going against me. Such as: A major Hollywood studio purchased my novel *Christy*, then decided not to produce it. The fiction manuscript on which I had been working was presenting massive problems. Soon it was apparent that after pouring myself into it for three years, I was going to have to abandon this particular book.

Not only that, but outside, external inconveniences came on in waves: the dishwasher went out, the bathroom plumbing went awry; a truck driver backed into our mailbox and demolished it; the lawn developed chinch bugs; the car kept stopping cold on us. Petty discouragements, except that they kept piling up.

My rebellion extended for a period of six months. I see it now as a rebellion against God because I felt He had betrayed me. "What *can* we believe about healing through prayer?" I asked with seething anger and doubt just under the surface.

Almost everyone has gone through the same inner struggle over what seems like an unnecessary death. "How can God permit such things to happen?" is the cry of our hearts. "If He is a loving God, surely He would not want such evils to befall us." Here I was a grandmother, and still I had not come to terms with one of the basic problems of evil in all religious inquiry.

Years before I had met this same issue in Hannah Whitall Smith's *The Christian's Secret of a Happy Life*. I had been able to accept and profit from all the rest of Hannah's book, but my rebellion was violent against chapter twelve, "Is God in Everything?" I asked myself how God could be "in" the death of a three-year-old who wandered into the street in the path of a truck? Was God in war? In cancer? The answer that welled up inside me was a resounding "Certainly not!"

Further, I even considered such submissiveness wrong when Christians confronted with such tragedies, intoned, "Then it must have been God's will" and quoted old harassed Job, "The Lord gave, and the Lord taketh away; blessed be the name of the Lord." To me this seemed an especially cruel and offensive form of piosity.

But Hannah Smith asserted that for believers there could be but one basic response to the evil we encounter—the Scriptural admonition repeated over and over in the Old Testament and New: "In *everything* give thanks: for this is the will of God in Christ Jesus concerning you."[3] And "everything," she insisted, did mean everything—bad things as well as good.

Hannah warned that unless we do accept the fact that God is in everything, we can know no contentment. For how can we accept or give thanks for what is less than good if we do not believe that God's shielding Presence has deliberately stepped aside to allow those forces to reach us? Even more, that His purpose in stepping aside is for good—not evil?

I had decided that while Hannah Smith fully accepted this thesis, it was not for me. I had convinced myself I was hanging the matter on a hook for further consideration. Practically speaking, this was simply rejection.

I stood against Hannah Smith's thesis from 1945 until 1972. Twenty-seven years!

Amy Catherine's death brought me back face to face with it again. His voice did get through to me: *I, your God, am in everything. The baby died, but Amy is with Me. And while she lived, she ministered to everyone who prayed for her. Are you too stubborn, too arrogant to see it, Catherine? Are you going to continue to live in darkness month after month?*

I am grateful that at that juncture my husband Len and two close friends, Freddie Koch and Virginia Lively, were stern with me. "You're wallowing in self-pity, Catherine," they told me. "That can't be right. The self-pity, (wounded pride, perhaps?) the questioning God's love—all of it is standing between you and God."

Virginia Lively leaned forward, looked deep into my eyes. "Remember, Catherine, the word the Lord gave me during the Amy Catherine crisis?"

Yes, I remembered. With ringing authority, Virginia had delivered to Peter and Edith a prophecy: "The Lord wants me to assure you that any other child you have, you can have with perfect confidence."

Several of us there were inclined to be suspicious of prophecy, wary of false prophets. But Virginia was an old and trusted friend with a valid continuing relationship with Jesus Christ. Could we really put our weight down on this hope?

"That prophecy still stands, Catherine," Virginia went on. "You've got to trust Jesus for the future, that He always *restores.*"

"But for now," Len's voice was very gentle, "if you'll only admit the self-pity and rebellion to Him, Catherine, He'll remove the cloud. I know He will."

They were right, of course. Finally on my knees, with a flood of tears, I made my confession. Then I saw that when life hands us situations which we cannot understand, we have one of two choices: we can wallow in misery, separated from God. Or we can tell Him, "I need You and Your presence in my life more than I need understanding. I choose You, Lord. I trust You to give me understanding and an answer to my 'Why?' if and when You choose."[4]

Sweet peace flowed into me, the first I had known in months. After that God took me back in my life to show me step by step how He had dealt with me through illness, death, lack of friends, loneliness. He *had* been with me in all of it.

Then I realized that it was Jesus Himself who in His timeless story of the Prodigal Son, gave us the best illustration of how eagerly He receives back any of us who

have turned away from Him. Here was a son who had
wandered far from his God-marked path.

With my rebellious spirit, I too had been adrift in a far
country. But like the Prodigal, the minute I turned around
and faced Home, I found God, my Father—more loving
even than my earthly father—running down the road to
meet me.

At that moment God's restoration work began.

When Edith and Peter told us two years later that they
were expecting their fourth child, knowing the history of
the two genetically-damaged babies, the obstetrician was
unable to give Edith any medical prognosis. She was to
find out later that the doctor himself had been on tenter-
hooks all during her pregnancy.

Fear kept rising unbidden to our minds despite Virginia
Lively's reassuring prophecy. It was a difficult time for all
of us, especially for Edith. Repeatedly she sought some
assurance from the Lord, but no direct word was
forthcoming.

Often during those days Edith found that she could
identify with the agony of the Psalmist David as he too
experienced the silence of Jehovah—God...

"How long, O Lord? Will you hide Yourself forever?[5]"

"Why," she wondered, "has God always required of
His children periods of enduring His silence, His inscrut-
ability? Is it simply that the limitations of our humanness
can never finally penetrate or comprehend the infinite
mind and purposes of God? Or are such periods—when
'the heavens being as brass'—a necessary part of teaching
us to trust God even in the dark?"

At last the long wait was over. Labor pains began on
the morning of May 4, 1974. A few hours later in the
delivery room at Goddard Memorial Hospital in Stough-

ton, Massachusetts, as a baby boy was born to Edith and Peter, the obstetrician began chuckling, then laughing. "Nothing wrong with *this* baby, Edith. He's *plenty* vigorous. Superstar muscle tone!"

A few minutes later, as the doctor almost bounded out of the room, he paused at the head of the delivery table. Very tenderly, holding Edith's face between his hands, his voice alive with feeling, he told her elatedly, "It's moments like that that make this business worthwhile."

So Virginia's prophecy was right. Peter Jonathan—robust, with irrepressible vitality and an exceptionally happy disposition, was to be the first of God's joyful surprises.

Left Side: Jeffrey, Chester, Linda, Lucille (seated), Leonard, Catherine
Right Side: (clockwise) Peter, Edith, Mary Elizabeth,
and Peter Jonathan Marshall, Leonora (Christy) Wood, and Prince

The
Road From
Here

....you will know them
by their fruits.
....he shall see the fruit
of the travail of His soul
and be satisfied....

Matthew 7:20; Isaiah 53:11

The Road From Here

The evening of August 18, 1979 Len and I waited expectantly in our bedroom at Evergreen Farm in Virginia. I was wearing an evening dress, he, a formal summer coat. The knock on the door came at 6:40 p.m. Len opened the door. Outside stood our grandchildren—Mary Elizabeth, 10, in a long dress, and Peter Jonathan, 5, in his Sunday suit.

"We came to escort you to the drawing-room," they announced with giggles.

Peter Jonathan reached up for my arm, Len took Mary's and we descended the stairs. At the bottom flashcubes popped. There the members of our family greeted us. Slim, dark-haired Chester, our 26-year-old son, called for silence and announced from a long scroll

"Hear Ye, Hear Ye, Hear Ye
Sarah Catherine Wood Marshall LeSourd
and
Leonard Earle LeSourd
having been joined in holy matrimony, lo, these 20

years, it is only fitting and proper that this august occasion be set aside to honor your union and its subsequent fruits.

Heretofore, be it known that the undersigned do express their heartfelt gratitude and admiration, acknowl-
edge their overwhelming debt, and pledge their loyalty,
love and service.

Delivered this 18th day of August, 1979, by

```
Leonora Whitaker Wood  .. Leonard Chester LeSourd
Edith Wallis Marshall .......... Jeffrey Alan LeSourd
Peter John Marshall ........ Mary Elizabeth Marshall
Linda Ann LeSourd ....... Peter Jonathan Marshall"
```

Thus began one of those family evenings you would like
to have on stop-action film so that you could rerun it over
and over. The actual date of our 20th anniversary was
November 14, 1979. Since the August date was when most
of the family could be together, it was chosen as a time
for something special—we were not told what.

Chester came from Chattanooga where he is an English
teacher and tennis coach at McCallie School. Jeff, 22, flew
in from Sikeston, Missouri, where he is a Bell Telephone
supervisor. Linda, 30, drove out from Washington where
she was working with young people for the National
Prayer Breakfast movement. The Marshall family had been
staying with us at the farm over the summer, bringing
together four generations of our family ranging in ages
from 5 to 87.

Secret preparations had begun early in the week. Brown
sacks filled with edibles were brought in and furtively
stashed away. The night before, two cars of family arrived
after Len and I had gone to bed. We heard muffled laughter
with many trips from the cars to the kitchen; lights were
still on well after midnight.

The next morning Len and I were told to stay away from
the refrigerator. No wonder! Odd, thumping noises were
coming from it. And green stuff—could it be seaweed?—

kept oozing out. Chester seemed to be the keeper of whatever was in there, faintly drumming. Nervously, he kept returning again and again to the refrigerator, keeping anxious vigil.

During the day several rehearsals were called from which we were excluded. Our children and grandchildren made it clear that today they were taking complete control of the household.

After we had assembled in the living room, the first course was served—steamed clams in large bowls along with melted butter. We moved to the dining room for the second course—delicate green salad served on crystal plates. The table was set with the best linen, crystal, and silver. My mother had ordered pink roses for the centerpiece, set off by tall, pink tapers.

Next came the stellar entrée—live lobsters flown in from Maine, then boiled. So live lobsters had been the refrigerator-thumpers. And that explained the oozing seaweed and Chester's great derring-do to keep the lobsters alive for 24 hours. When corn on the cob and fresh asparagus with hollandaise sauce were served, it was obvious why questions about our favorite foods had been put to us weeks before. The meal-end fillip: Baked Alaska with raspberry sauce.

The evening's finale was another surprise. "Now we're ready to have the full story of how you met—and your courtship," Linda instructed us, as everyone around the table pushed their chairs back to find a comfortable position.

"We want a description of the first kiss, when you knew you were in love—every last detail," Jeff continued unabashedly.

A surprised look crossed Len's face, reflecting my reaction too. "You kids can't be serious! Why would you be interested in personal details like that?"

"Oh, but we *are!*" It was a chorus.

"Come on, Dad! Tell it all," Chester prodded. "Only *not* all those old stories about what brats we were—like my sliding spinach off my plate and tossing it behind the radiator in the kitchen."

"Oh, let's have those too," Mary Elizabeth bubbled.

"Also tell us," Edith suggested, "what you consider some of the most important lessons you've learned over the past twenty years."

As I sat there looking around the table, into my mind played back some words I had written in 1961 as part of the Foreword for my book *Beyond Our Selves*:

> Len's three children have joined Peter John in calling me "Mother"... Many experiences have tested me in my lifetime, but none more than this one. And none has made me happier. But writing about it must come later. *A man swimming a horse across a turbulent stream does not stop to take a picture of the experience. I'll get my colts across the stream, see them thoroughly dried off, well fed and on their way—then perhaps, the picture.*

Eighteen tempestuous, crowded, fulfilling years had passed since I had penned those words. Gratitude welled up in me as I thought of the One who had been with us all the way to see us safely across the rough crossing. And here the colts were, not only dried off and on their way, but for this evening, having taken charge of their parents with competent maturity.

And so for the rest of the evening Len and I covered the highlights of courtship and twenty years of marriage including many of the stories recounted in this book. It was an unforgettable evening of sharing between four generations of family...

A new experience in communal living had begun in November, 1977 when Peter had resigned from his church

in East Dennis, Massachusetts, after ministering there for
eleven years. He and his family had then moved temporarily into the house next to ours in Florida while Peter
continued his nationwide preaching and teaching ministry, awaiting a new call from the Lord.

At that time the family stretched all the way from Peter
Jonathan, age three, and Mary Elizabeth, almost eight, to
my mother, their great-grandmother, 87. Our plan had
been to retain the two smaller family units for breakfasts
and lunches but have communal evening meals, alternat-
ing between the two homes.

As time went on the dinner hour remained the reporting
and clearing center for the day's events and for the
thoughts, insights, and problems we wanted to share.
Most of the time the dilemma was getting in a word edge-
wise. This proved especially frustrating to Peter Jonathan,
to whom we promised to set aside a chink of time so that
even his "news" could be heard.

Typically, a ten-year-old Mary Elizabeth might report
what she had learned in school that day about chlorophyll
in leaves of plants and about the distributive property of
multiplication. Her blue eyes would sparkle as she en-
thused over her horseback riding lesson... "I learned to
post." And could one of us please help her wallpaper
another room of her miniature dollhouse?

Len was doing what he loves most: nurturing and build-
ing a Christian work from a small beginning. First, it was
Guideposts; now it was the Chosen Books Publishing
Company.

Peter's book, written with David Manuel, *The Light and
the Glory,* had sold 80,000 plus copies...

That day ten eager women had come to my mother's
weekly, home Bible study on the epistles of John.

Recreation was an important lubricant for this extended
family life. Such fun as Peter teaching Peter Jonathan how
to throw a ball and swing a baseball bat; swimming lessons;
handicrafts; Peter Jonathan and Mary Elizabeth learning

correct tennis from their grandfather Len; family tennis doubles; Peter Jonathan and Mary Elizabeth cuddled up to Len, one on each side of him, listening spellbound to one of their grandfather's "Lucky stories."

Lucky stories are now a family tradition, first told to Chester and Jeffrey when they were small. Wild tales of suspense, always in exotic settings, with a man named "Lucky" as the hero, the story always containing a moral. Len spins out the plot as he goes along. He claims that this talent for instant story plots stems from having read shelf after shelf of every *Tom Swift, Rover Boy* type of series books while he was growing up.

Invariably today's chapter ends with Lucky in a tough spot, hanging by his fingertips over a pool of hungry crocodiles, or about to be trapped by thugs as Lucky plunges deeper and deeper into the shaft of an old mine.

Then too, games have always been a big part of family recreation: *Rook* and croquet and *Parcheesi* and bridge and, of course, *Geography*.

This is a favorite after-dinner game enjoyed by all four generations and any and all guests present. Paper and pencil are handed out; two teams choose up; a letter of the alphabet such as "P" is selected; take five minutes in which to write down any town, city, mountain, lake, river, etc. anywhere in the world beginning with "P."

Mary Elizabeth's paper is always studded with every hamlet and pond on Cape Cod. Mother's is invariably loaded with those outlandishly remote places from the Great Smoky "Christy country" she knows so well, like Persimmon Hill, Pebble Mountain, or Pigeon Roost Hollow. Len, who has played this game since he was a boy, usually comes out on top as the sophisticated *Geography* expert.

Scoring is simple. Each person reads his list aloud. With six people playing, if Mother, for instance, is the only one with "Pebble Mountain," then she gets six for that; if all six have it, each scores only one. The winning team is the one with the most points.

Geography is always highly competitive (heated discussions such as whether "Chesapeake" is a bay or a peninsula), educational and fun, often hilarious.

Then, as in all extended families, there are those special affinities that develop person to person. What *is* that special bond between Peter Jonathan and his great-grandmother "Nana"? Who can tell! Is it that age has dropped out a lot of false values and finally retains the imperishables—a childlike imagination and faith?

Almost any afternoon about four o'clock would find Peter Jonathan marching in the back door with favorite books under his arm, after which he and Nana would sit close together at one end of the davenport or in the lounge chair in her bedroom. She has read her way through stacks of juveniles, told her great-grandson the wonderful Old Testament stories, and begun to help him memorize the Catechism for Young Children.

Who but Peter Jonathan could have succeeded in turning his great-grandmother into his helicopter co-pilot? Edith walked in on them one evening to find her son sitting squeezed in beside Nana in her armchair. A baseball bat lay in front of them resting on both arms of the chair. Nana, instructed to hold on tightly to the "safety bar" with one hand, was looking a little sheepish.

"We're playing 'helicopter'," Peter told his mother. "I'm the pilot, Nana's the co-pilot."

"Are you old enough to fly a helicopter?"

"Yes, we're both 158 years old, and Mommie..." the five-year-old pointed out the picture window to the full moon in the sky, "Nana told me about the man in the moon. Somebody forgot and left him there. We're goin' fly up there and bring him back."

There are many pluses and blessings for extended families such as ours has been for this three-and-a-half-year period. Among them, the obvious advantage of always having someone around for baby-sitting and child care; always someone to read or tell stories to the children or to play games; always someone for the mending and the darning, for the household baking or to prepare vegetables for dinner, to make special desserts, even perhaps a big freezer of homemade peach or strawberry ice cream.

When I was growing up, it was a usual thing for families to include a grandparent, an uncle or aunt, or an unmarried daughter or a bachelor son. Sociological facts verify this: In the 1920s 50 percent of the households in Massachusetts, for instance, included at least one adult other than both parents. Today that figure is only four percent.

The change in family life today is startling. Now not only is the extended family a rarity; even the intact nuclear family is becoming the exception. Divorce is so epidemic (one million divorces a year in the United States with the figure rising rapidly) that the number of children now living with only one parent approaches 40 percent. This one parent at home is usually the mother, and increasingly, she is not there either because she is working. One of the effects of "women's liberation" is that between 1947 and 1975 the number of working wives shot up 205 percent. Even for mothers with tiny children under three, one in three is now working. And judges in divorce courts are finding an increasing number of cases where neither parent wants custody of the children.

Behind all this is a rampant "me-first" philosophy. Endlessly, we are hearing about the "rights of the individual." The question then becomes, does solitary, self-centered living really enable one to find oneself? *Does* selfishness bring happiness and fulfillment?

Our experiment in communal living has shed much light on these crucial questions, for four generations cannot live together without rubbings. In that lovely verse from the

Psalms,[1] we are told that "God sets the solitary in families." Now we know why: He knows, if we do not, that every husband and every wife are "incompatible"; all parents are "incompatible" with all children. So what does that prove? Only that the Creator made each human being a distinctly unique individual.

That being so, in the first years of life, each of us needs the nuturing love and also the discipline of the smaller nuclear family unit before being plunged into the rough hurly-burly of community life. And so He has ordained the family as society's most important unit and as its finest proving ground and character training school for us to learn how to handle our uniqueness.

So we found it. The rubbing and scraping often produced a crisis. God's way is not to flee the crisis but to uncover the root of it and so a growing edge of the inner spirit. As we handled problems together in prayer, we surrendered yet another layer of selfishness and subsequently grew in maturity.

For instance, my mother frantically called to Edith one afternoon, "Quick! Get Peter Jonathan down. He's climbed almost to the top of the big mango tree."

Edith's response was calm. "Gram, it's all right for him to climb trees."

We were learning that the same "Christy" who, at 19, traveled alone into the wild Great Smokies, walked seven miles through the snow with the mailman to get to Cutter's Gap, was a daring horse-woman, and faced down moonshiners, now approaching 90—has many fears as she looks about her at our world.

That night at dinner the heart of the question was submitted: How many of my mother's fears were the wisdom of age and therefore legitimate? Or could we be in danger of passing on to children a fear-filled attitude to life?

The discussion grew heated. The woman who so many years before had swept majestically into Mr. Rush Hazen's office, flaunting her big-plumed hat, the same one who had stood off the roughest mountaineers, can still be fiery: she could not help her fears for the children's safety and thought them legitimate.

"But," Edith protested, "it isn't that I want any life-threatening danger for my child..."

"Isn't falling out of a high tree life-threatening?" Mother shot back, sparks in her eyes.

"I want my son to have the freedom to climb and run, to have some rough and tumble," Peter interjected. "Children, especially boys, can't be protected from all danger and hurt, Grandmother."

Almost always our give-and-take sessions end up in prayer for the wisdom of God's specific direction for the problem and for the right attitude in each of us. For throughout these years we have found prayer the best lubricant of all—in fact, indispensable.

As in all families, selfishness, jealousy, haughtiness, anger erupt at times. If it comes from a child, then there is correction; if from an adult, we gather together to pray it through, letting the Helper—the Holy Spirit—do the correcting. It is amazing how often He does, with gentle incisiveness.

Like most people I resist criticism; my defenses go up quickly when I see it coming even though I know it is essential to Christian growth. The reason I cannot slough off my wrongdoing is that the price of setting it right came so high—even to God Himself. Jesus went to the cross to make possible the Father's forgiveness for me, for everyone of us—past, present, and future.

But we Christians have heard these words so often that, like well-worn coins, they slip through our fingers. On a certain morning several years ago, God graciously made them shining and new for me.

It was during a period when an awareness of my own mistakes and wrong turnings had given me a sense of isolation from God. As I sat in a living room chair pondering this, there came to me a deep interior experience.

I did not fall asleep, so this was no dream. Nor was it an otherworldly "vision." It seemed real, as real as the fabric on the chair, or the Florida sunlight pouring through the windows or the trilling of a mockingbird in a ficus tree outside. Suddenly, I felt the presence of Jesus.

"We're going on a journey," He told me.

Soon we were in a long, long room, like a throne room. Crowds of people lined the walls on either side. As we walked the length of the room approaching One whom I knew to be God, the Father, I spotted in the crowd those I love who have gone on before: my father who died in 1961, Peter Marshall, and my grandson, Peter Christopher—now not a baby, but a tall, slim, thirteen-year-old. There was my granddaughter, Amy Catherine, a delightful little girl.

Then I looked down at myself: to my horror I was dressed in rags—torn, unwashed, filthy. How could I bear to stand before the Father, the Lord God Omnipotent, clothed so vilely? When we stopped before the throne, I could not even look up. I had never felt so unworthy.

In the same instant Jesus spread wide the voluminous robe He was wearing, completely covering me with it. (Interestingly, this was no kingly robe, rather the roughest homespun material. I understood that until all His children are brought to glory, He continues to wear the robe of His humanity.)

"Now," He told me, "My father does not see you at all—only Me. Not your sins but My righteousness. I cover for you."

Then I was aware again of the living room and the chair, only now feelings of joy and gratitude were washing over me. So that's what the Cross means! The theologians have a high-sounding phrase for it—"substitutionary atonement." Jesus in our place. Jesus our substitute. Jesus covering for us.

Even though I'm now a grandmother, I know more clearly than ever that I'm still as needy and dependent on the Lord's help as when I was a child, first hearing His voice. He has allowed me to go off on selfish tangents and wander down wrong paths, but always He meets me at every turn and brings me back to Him.

Two new members have been added to our family in the past year: Susan Scott, whom I described earlier as Chester's lovely new wife, and Philip Lader, now Linda's husband.

On the evening of September 19, 1980 at Linda's and Philip's rehearsal dinner in the dining room of Fellowship House in Washington, D. C., the cooks and waitresses were Linda's friends, part of a small Washington "fellowship family," as she called it. Among impromptu speech-toasts after dessert were those of Jim Hiskey, a professional golfer, a sort of chaplain to athletes, a man who has been training young people in Christian discipleship for over twenty years. He had been our daughter's first boss in Washington. Len and I listened, fascinated, as Jim described the Linda he had first seen and her subsequent development... "Chunky, long straight hair, granny glasses. I needed a secretary. I remember the first letter I tried to dictate to Linda." Jim paused and chuckled. "There must have been, oh, thirty-odd mistakes on the first typed page.

"But then I watched Jesus Christ slowly transform a girl, rub off the rough edges, develop the potential deep within her. I saw the unfolding of a lovely young woman, like a rosebud opening in the sunshine.

"Only that development made possible what we are celebrating here tonight. I knew that this new Linda was going to need a strong husband. Well, she's about to have one. Because Philip Lader is an achiever and an idealist if I ever saw one. He's earned his own way from the be-ginning—through Duke University, Harvard Law School,

Oxford University, a bachelor until 34. But I don't think he would have fallen for the first Linda we knew."

Jim's comments were dramatized for Len and me two days later during the wedding at the National Presbyterian Church. The setting—the jewel-colors of the tall, stained-glass windows complimented by the rose red of the brides-maids' dresses and the brilliant vestments of the two cler-gymen. The two grandmothers—Lucile LeSourd and my mother, Leonora Wood rolled down the long aisle in their wheelchairs; Phil's widowed mother, Mary Lader, and his aunt, Eleanor Tripoli, beaming from the other side of the aisle. They had been praying for Philip's future wife for many years, they had confided.

We kept catching echoes of Peter's and Edith's wedding 15 years before, since this too was not just a marriage ceremony, but a worship service as well. There was con-gregational singing, two portions of scripture read by friends of Linda's and Phil's, the bride and groom kneeling together, taking communion as the first act of their married life.

This service also included something new to most of us. Just prior to the traditional wedding vows, Linda and Phil faced one another, while each pledged to the other vows they themselves had written. There was an astonishing meld of a romantic idealism centered in the love of God along with a clear-eyed grasp of the responsibilities being assumed.

Phil's deeply resonant voice began,

> "Linda, after our first moments together, I prayed that you would one day be my wife. You caused me to understand that man's way to joy is a remarkable love. The 'I will' said today is not so much fact accom-plished, as responsibility assumed....

> "You and I are commissioned by this wedding to make God's love believable to the world.

> By His grace however, we have different gifts, and

these beg quarrels. When frustrated by your tenacity of opinion, I shall not waive my own,"—ripple of laughter over the congregation—"but shall honestly and patiently seek resolution....

"My acceptance of you and your freckles is unconditional. There will *never* be a price of admission to my heart.

"However poetic this view of marriage, I promise always to be an idealist. But an idealist without illusions. I ask you to challenge us to practice the presence of God.

"My marriage proposal in a tree house was to symbolize what little material security I can offer you. We shall not fear to risk our prosperity for the principles and dreams we share. I shall thereby shield you from the leprosy of boredom and convention....

"I shall heed the lilies of the field to make time for us amidst the clamor of events....To watch sunsets, to call dolphins. Let's laugh at ourselves and together strive for a riper, more delicious happiness than we have ever known....

"I commit to you that ours will be a death in love and not a death of love; that in the evening of our lives, the joy will have been worth the pain....

"That sun will all too quickly set on our lives. But even then as your husband and as a Christian, I shall— and here Phil's voice trembled and broke—*never* say good-by."

As Linda, looking radiantly beautiful, began to speak before the hushed church, Len and I found out later that we were having much the same thoughts. That first morning of our coffee-pot experiment 21 years before, we had struggled to find the right prayer for Linda. At that time the problem seemed to be how to get this talented girl moving in the direction God had for her.

In a special sense, what was unfolding before us that afternoon was as though God were placing in our hands the golden crown of Answered Prayer—indeed, of countless prayers melded in the furnace of His love.

As we watched Linda, her blue eyes looking deep into Phil's hazel eyes, pouring out the desires of her heart to him, we knew that never had a dream been so gloriously fulfilled.

> "Phil, I not only love you, I respect you. I'm honored to become your wife today. I desire always to be an encouragement to you, and I want to provide a haven and a resting place for you and for our children.
>
> "I promise to speak and live the truth in love with you to the best of my ability. At times that may be painful for one or both of us. Yet I, too, am committed to work through any differences that arise with love, understanding and resolution as our goal. And I promise to uphold and stand by you always....
>
> "I am excited about what lies ahead, a bit overwhelmed by the enormity and the irrevocability of the commitment we are making. But open-eyed, counting the cost and exulting in the assurance we both have of the rightness of this covenant, I will walk with you through the challenging and glorious future God has for us...".

Our eyes moved to Mary Elizabeth Marshall, the junior bridesmaid, standing with the group around the altar listening. Len and I saw much the same starry-eyed look on her face we had seen on Linda's at Peter's and Edith's wedding. Even so, He passes on His great love and His incredible idealism from generation to generation.

Edith could not be there to see her daughter, for she was in Florida expecting the addition of the next member of our family any moment.

Three days later, on September 24, David Christopher Marshall was born, a healthy beautiful baby. Because this was "natural" childbirth, Peter was there standing at the head of the delivery table to encourage and to help Edith, to cradle his son in his arms minutes after he was born.

And so once again, Virginia Lively's beautiful prophecy of healthy babies for the Marshalls was fulfilled—as indeed, all of our Father's promises are eventually worked out for us.

Goodness and mercy shall follow you all the days of your life. This had been His pledge to me on that dark day of Peter Marshall's death as I was about to leave the little hospital room with my life lying in shambles about me. "Goodness and mercy"...*His* goodness. *His* mercy. How bounteously He has honored His pledge to me.

Sometimes we have to lift our eyes to the hills to get His perspective, wait for what seems to us earthbound creatures a long time to see the fulfillment of His promises.

But this I have learned—we can trust Him.

Life Principles

Chapter six

When life caves in, we are to seek God in our problem. God has a plan for every life by which He will bring good out of evil.

Chapter seven

We should never hesitate to try the impossible. God does have a special work for us to do in the world. Should this involve a big dream, we must believe that the bigger the dream, and the more loving and unselfish it is, the greater will be God's blessing on it.

Chapter eight

God has special promises and provision for all those single parents who must rear children alone. We are not to clutch our children to ourselves. What we hold too tightly, we can drive away or break. When we give our children up to God, He will eventually give them back to us.

Chapter nine

Since God made us for companionship, loneliness is not His plan for us. But there is a price to be paid in seeking God's remedy, not ours. This includes a decision to give up self-pity, the determination not to compromise honor and purity and idealism, and the willingness to let Him fill our heart's lonely places with His love which can then spill out into loving concern for others.

Chapter ten

God is forever in the repair and restoration business. When we are willing to be taught by Him and to make Him the center of the new home, He will produce love and harmony and joy as He fits together the pieces of two broken households.

Chapter eleven

Husbands and wives are basically incompatible. Parents are incompatible with their children. God made us all different. That's why the home is His classroom for moulding and shaping us into mature people.

Chapter twelve

God uses children and grandchildren to keep older people flexible. When anyone of us has a painful experience that our mind cannot equate with a loving God, there is this remedy: "I want You and Your presence, Lord, even more than I want understanding. I choose You." When we ask this, He then gives peace and illumination as His gift.

Notes

Chapter 1   Our Father Who Art on Earth
1. Judges 16:30

Chapter 3   My God Was Too Small
1. J. Middleton Murray, *Journal of Katherine Mansfield* (London: Constable, 1927). Used by permission of Alfred A. Knopf, Inc., and the Society of Authors as the Literary Representative of the late Miss Katherine Mansfield.

Chapter 4   Romance
1. O. Hallesby, *Prayer* (Translated by Clarence J. Carlsen) (Minneapolis, Minnesota: Augsburg Publishing House, 1931, 1960), p. 17. Used by permission.

Chapter 5   Illness

1. Exodus 15:26	4. Isaiah 55:11	7. Luke 4:12
2. Isaiah 53:4,5	5. Luke 4:9	8. John 5:39 *(RSV)*
3. James 5:14,15	6. Luke 4:10	9. Joel 2:28; Acts 2:17

Chapter 6   Grief

1. Isaiah 66:13	3. Isaiah 61:1,3
2. John 14:18	4. Proverbs 15:25

5. Jeremiah 49:11   James Moffatt, *The Bible, A New Translation* (New York: Harper & Row, 1935)

6. Isaiah 54:4,6,7,13
An especially encouraging translation of verse 13 is worth noting here: "All your sons will be taught *by* the Lord, and great shall be your children's peace." *(New International Version)*, italics added.

7. Isaiah 41:10 *(The Amplified Bible)*	10. Luke 23:42,43
8. Hebrews 2:15 *(The Amplified Bible)*	11. I Corinthians 15:42-44
9. I Corinthians 13:12	

Chapter 7   His Call to Me

1. Romans 8:28	2. I John 5:14,15	3. Matthew 6:33

4. Originally from one of Peter Marshall's "Postscripts" in a church bulletin...Quoted also in: Peter Marshall, *Mr. Jones, Meet the Master* (Westwood, NJ: Fleming H. Revell Company, 1949), p. 34

5. Catherine Marshall, *To Live Again* (New York: McGraw-Hill Book Company, 1957), p. 54. (Lincoln, Va.: Chosen Books, 1979), p. 54.

6. Ibid, p. 53

Chapter 8   Single Parent

1. Acts 6:1	3. Genesis 9:16
2. James 1:27	4. Matthew 28:20

Chapter 11   Second Family

1.   Mark 11:25,26 *(Revised Standard Version)*

2.   I Peter 2:24 *(The Amplified Bible)*

3.   See the following chapter for the outcome.

Chapter 12   Grandmother

1.   Margaret Prescott Montague, *Twenty Minutes of Reality, The Atlantic Monthly* (November, 1916)

2.   Genesis 2:19   3.   I Thessalonians 5:18

4.   Here I was merely learning for myself the important lessons thousands of Christians before me have had to come to. Succinctly expressed by the seventeenth century Brother Lawrence:

> "….a sharp distinction should be drawn between acts of the understanding and those of the will—that the former were of small account and the latter, everything…."

Brother Lawrence, *The Practice of the Presence of God* (New York: Paulist Press, 1978), p. 72.

5.   Psalm 89:46 *(The Amplified Bible)*

Scripture references

Chapter 1

1.   Judges 16:30

Chapter 5

1.   Exodus 15:26

2.   Isaiah 53:4,5

3.   James 5:14-15

4.   Luke 4:9

5.   Luke 4:10

6.   Luke 4:12

7.   John 5:39-40 *(RSV)*

Chapter 6

1.   Isaiah 66:12-13

2.   John 14:18

3.   Isaiah 61:1,3

4.   Proverbs 15:25

5.   Jeremiah 49:11 *(Moffatt)*

6.   Isaiah 54:4,6,7,13

7.   Isaiah 41:10 *(Amplified)*

8.   Hebrews 2:15

9.   I Corinthians 13:12

10.   Luke 23:42-43

11.   I Corinthians 15:42-44

Chapter 7

1.   Romans 8:28

2.   I John 5:14-15

3.   Matthew 6:33

Chapter 8

1.   Acts 6:1 *(RSV)*

2.   James 1:27 *(RSV)*

3.   Genesis 9:16

4.   Matthew 28:20

Chapter 11

1.   Mark 11:25-26

2.   I Peter 2:24 *(Amplified)*

Chapter 12

1.   Genesis 2:19

2.   Psalm 89:46 *(Amplified)*